DEAR WALLFLOWER

Bambina Dear

Dear Wallflower

Published by Starlily
An imprint of Dearverse Publishing
Trade names of Dearverse Media Productions, operated by Bambina Dear
San Antonio, Texas

www.dearversemedia.com

This book is a dramatized and poetic retelling of real events from the author's life. While certain details have been adapted for storytelling purposes, it remains a deeply personal reflection of lived experiences.

ISBN: 979-8-9926781-0-9

Cover and illustrations created using Canva Pro elements. Some design elements are sourced from Canva's licensed content.

About Dearverse Media Productions

Dearverse Media Productions is an independent storytelling house dedicated to crafting immersive narratives across multiple art forms. Founded by Bambina Dear, we specialize in evocative, thought-provoking stories that blend poetry, visual art, and cinematic storytelling.

At Dearverse, we believe that stories have the power to shape worlds—both on the page and on the screen. Our mission is to create deeply resonant works that challenge, inspire, and connect audiences through bold, unconventional storytelling.

For updates on upcoming releases, exclusive content, and behind-the-scenes insights, visit @DearverseMediaPro on all social media platforms.

Trigger Warning

This book contains references to drug use, sexual assault, suicidal ideation, and mental health struggles.

Dear Wallflower,

If you see yourself in these pages
do not be discouraged.

We've all been through phases
accepting love we don't deserve.

We fight through spiritual warfare
to find our inner peace.

We grow with every season
and won't stop until
we're free.

CHAPTERS

Flowers

Are joy
Bring joy
Take joy

Wait a second

Flowers

We
Plant them
Pluck them
Mow them down
Pass them around
Ignore them
To death

Sigh
(because what a shame)

Pulverize them
Until they're something else

Silence
(because somehow that's worse)

Flowers
Are resilient

INTRO

Flowers
Are brilliant

They turn bullshit into energy
And energy into sustenance

Flowers
Can be sour
But

Flowers
Have power

To heal you
To harm you
To inebriate you
To cleanse you

To make you smile

Flowers

Deserve more than we give them.

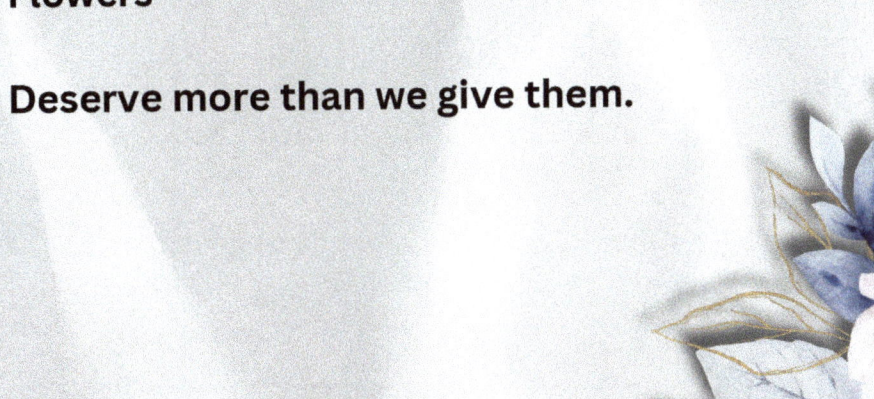

Dear Wallflower,

I promise there are
perks to growing tall.

They were hidden in messages
you never saw.
Parallel and perpendicular
to your favorite wall.

Waiting on you, reaching for you
Whispering your name

"Wallflower, Wallflower,
Gently
go insane."

Disappointment
Turns out the grass isn't greener
On their side
I tried to warn you
I guess it must've
Slipped your mind
Be patient, bite your tongue
Wait for the right moment
To punch then say
"**B**!^@# **F***@% you I'm done!"

Sometimes everything
Is what it seems
And some days
You'll be the cool fools queen

For now do your thing girl
Right now this is your world
You only have so many years to
To be young and wild
Only so much time
Before lifes toughest trials

Wallflower

Place to place
From face to face
I've seen and I've heard
Of people having their cake and eating it too
Round and round
From crowd to crowd
They phased me in and phased me out

I asked them
How do you do it
Teach me, make me better
How do you do it
Become a diamond, lasting forever

They told me not to be fooled
That no one truly has it all together
They've been lying so long
They forgot the cake in their palms

I think I've found my place among these high lives
Every gems a diamond under false light
We either fake it till we make it
Or we'll die trying

These are the perks of being someone that you don't like

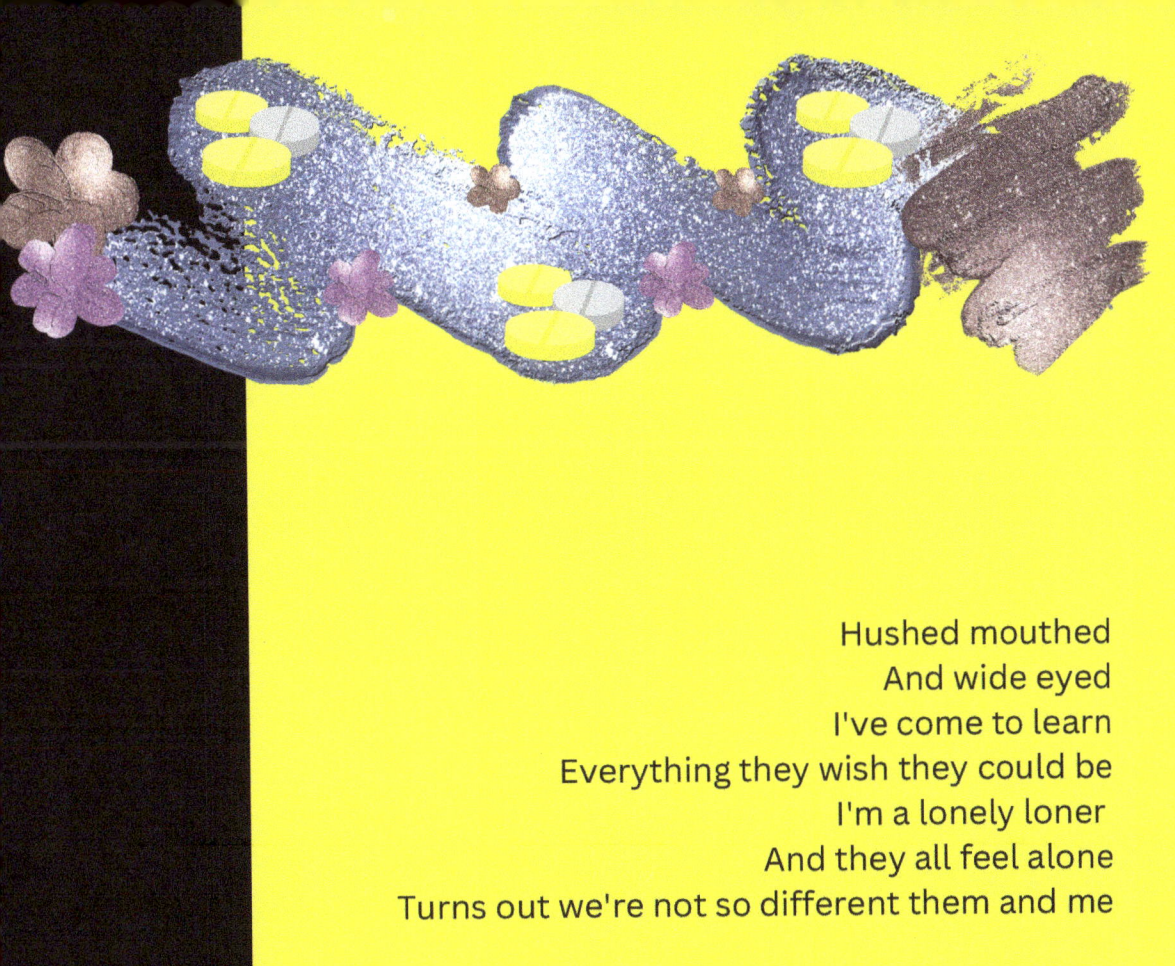

Hushed mouthed
And wide eyed
I've come to learn
Everything they wish they could be
I'm a lonely loner
And they all feel alone
Turns out we're not so different them and me

So I asked them, why do you live like this
Why hide realness in the background
I asked them to show me their truth
Are you a diamond or a rhinestone

They gave me a pitiful look
Like they were afraid to shatter a child
And they said
Being yourself won't always turn the profits
An unpreferable plight
But there's always a cost to feeling alive

I thought I found my place among these high lives
You know every gems a diamond under false light
We either fake it till we make it or we'll die trying

Here's a perc' for every part of you, you don't like

Feel The Vibe

Feel the vibe
Listen to it
Respect
Take a breath
Touch my body
Touch me heart
Touch my head
Breath into me
A feeling so amazing
I see the face of God in the sky
Get me high
I can almost reach the dynamo
When we vibe
Get me high
Tell me when you can feel
Your lungs quivering with the vibe
Get me high
So far up I'm now one
With the heavenly sky

Our elders wonder
Why we're so extreme
But they were no different
We're all just searching for
Something to get that lifted
feeling

It doesn't have to be a drug
Don't have to be a crime
It doesn't have to mean
Putting your life on the line

But it's whatever
Do what ever you wanna do
Howl to the moon
They'll still pray
Angels take pity on you
Show you the truth

Or
At least a partial one to make
You see it all different
Question life
Maybe switch up positions

But a flock of y'all just sheep
Following the heard blindly
That religion ain't no joke
Don't laugh
Don't take it lightly
Mean that politely

And I don't mean to be
All Debby on your high
Get it?
It's just the shit
I think about when I vibe
Get me high

Come over here
Feel my vibe
Hear the women
Howl like wolves in the night
Feel my vibe
My homes the sky
My address is cloud 9

The struggle's only temporary

It's a phase girl

Dry your eyes it's not the end of the world

That shit that's on your mind

It isn't worth your time

Always steady stressing about the things we lose to fires

This part is only temporary

It's a phase girl

Dry your eyes

You have so much more to give the world

Beauty in the Sky

From the dust of the stars
To the sun burning bright
I can feel our energy
Melting the skies
Changing the vibe
From the homes of the rich and lit
To dark alley ways and sketchy strays
They're all the same
Beauty has many names
But darling so do the wicked
The troubled and insecure
Tell me what is the difference
Because from my point of You
Wicked can be beautiful
And they say
There's beauty in the break down
Maybe that's why
God made life
So hard

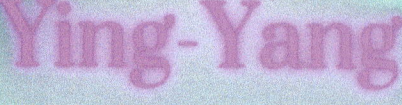

Ying-Yang

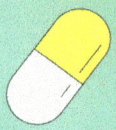

I got addictions
Running up the ying-yang:
Lovers, friends and alcohol
Parties, drugs, and light rain

I got addictions
running up the ying-yang
They're totally savage
They're wrecking their havoc

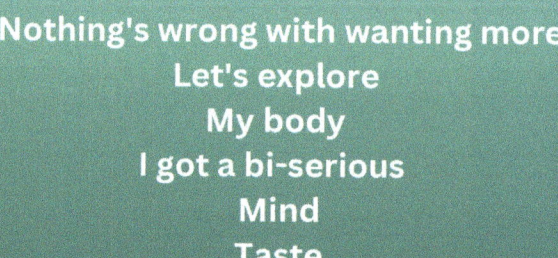

Nothing's wrong with wanting more
Let's explore
My body
I got a bi-serious
Mind
Taste
Fetish
For the boys who don't treat me right
Craving
For girls who think I'm theirs beyond tonight

I'm starting a collection of lovers
Each one's unique
Each one means a little less to me
And I can't let go
Each body I covet is dark mark on my soul

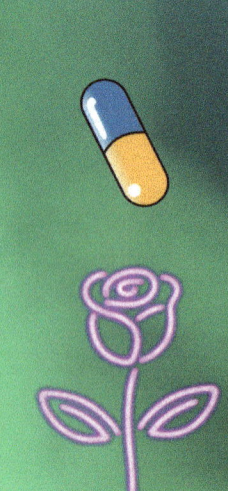

I got addictions
Running up the ying-yang:
Lovers, friends, and alcohol
Parties, drugs, and light rain

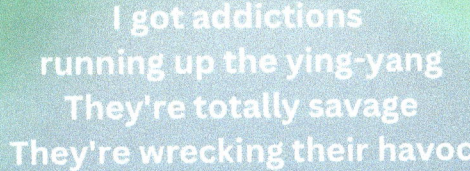
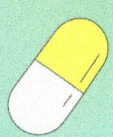

I got addictions
running up the ying-yang
They're totally savage
They're wrecking their havoc

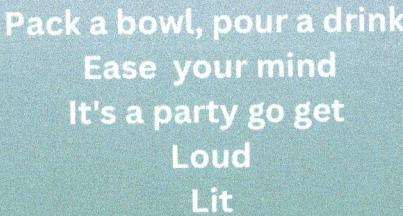

Pack a bowl, pour a drink
Ease your mind
It's a party go get
Loud
Lit

You're free to be whoever you want tonight
Check your worries at the door
Leave the struggle behind
Say "I can get fucked up if I wanna!
I can pop this pill if I wanna!
I'm gon' shake my ass cus I want to!
No need for saving nigga,
don't come to my rescue..."

Because nights like this
Are few and far between and laced with bliss
I cant let go
This lifestyle's having an adverse effect on my soul

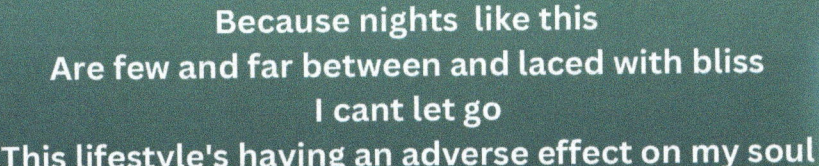

I got addictions
Running up the ying-yang
Lovers, friends, and alcohol
Parties, drugs, and light rain

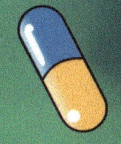

I got addictions
running up the ying-yang
They're totally savage
They're wrecking their havoc

Roulette

Wait
Something ain't right
Something ain't right
Something in these drugs made my chest too tight
1 minute 2 minute 3 minute 4
How long till someone finds me laid out on the floor
Aaaaah
It's easing up now
Body starts feeling like I'm on a cloud
Almost everything makes since now
And what I can't comprehend
Has to get the hell out
School has to go
Love has to go
There's a gun to my future
Should I let it go
Add a little something new to my regimen
Eeny meeny miny mo
Gamble with my fate again

It's that moment when the high kicks in.
Or is it low?
I don't know but I feel it down below,
And up above.
It's clouded my mind, it's weighed down my eyes,
It's got my body trembling;
And now I think in form of questions.

Where does my soul begin?
Are you a figment of imagination?
Is there more to this life?
Would it matter if I died right now?
Could you take away the hurt somehow?
Am I being punished?
Am I deserving?
Do I only exist to be his nothing?

It's that moment when the high kicks in.
Or is it low?
I don't know but I feel it down below,
And up above.
It's clouded my mind, it's weighed down my eyes,
It's got my body trembling;
And now I think in form of reasons.

The reason I get high every night to a different drug.
The reason that I cry, that bleed, that I've given up.
The reason I became who I am today.
The reason I've allowed my art to decay.
The reason behind every suicidal thought in my mind.
The reason I have yet to cross that line.

It's that moment when the high kicks in,
Or is it low?
I don't know but I feel it down below,
And up above.
It's clouded my mind, it's weighed down my eyes,
It's got my body trembling;
And now my thinking isn't lucid...

High Thought

27

May 2016

I could sit in a dark, abandoned room and be perfectly content for days at a time. Things like hunger wouldn't affect me. Strange, I know, but I don't feel like much of a person as of late. Rather, I feel like the emptiness that fills the room, leaving it cold, dank, and questionable.

On day five of absolute nothingness, I may venture outside my self-inflicted solitary confinement in search of company... sort of. I do not need, nor do I want, a companion to ensconce with me in my shabby corner. I don't want someone to talk to. Moving my jaw and forming words to practice the art of conversation seems like too much work for my semi-deranged mindset to process.

So, no. I don't want a cellmate in my homemade prison. The thought of someone even looking at me makes me anxious. I'm afraid they'll look too long, see too much. Perhaps see a glimmer of the girl that used to be here. But that glimmer is just a shadow, a falsified memory, and I know better than anyone that that girl no longer embodies this house.

When I leave this room, it will be to see how the outside world has moved on without me—to witness the subtle changes in my apartment made by my roommates. I'll sit outside on my balcony and gaze upon my neighbors and friends living life, only to sneak back to the safety of my room before anyone returns home.

When I open my door again and shakily make my way to the living room at midnight, it's to make sure I still have the option of company. I'll say hi to my friends and force myself to converse for a few minutes. A few days later, I'll repeat this cycle to make sure that when day twenty comes and the depression and anxiety are too much to bear, I still have these friends to pull a splinter of me back to reality.

When I seek company then return to my solitude, it's because I want to be alone but never lonely.

Moon Shine

A peculiar thing,
the moon drifted down from the sky
and whispered gently in my ear.

"Why do you cry? "

She kissed the tears on each of my cheeks,
gazing at me with a smile,
the sadness in her eyes mirroring my own.

I tilted my head as though to answer her question
until I caught a glance of the clock on the wall
and began to weep harder than before.

"No one stays," I mumbled.

The moon paused.
"That's a matter of perspective," she said;
as she sunk down and the sun rose over the horizon.

Phases
Do you know the meaning
Do you ever wonder if that next breath's worth repeating
Phases
There's more behind the meaning
In life we'll all experience the five stages or grieving
Phases
She's in hysterical denial
Cracking under pressure steady swearing
she's alright though
Phases
Bargain all you want to
Giving all of you away will never ever make him love you
Phases
Identify your true friends
Some are momentary be them lessons or convenience
Phases
Don't give up on the family
No one's picture perfect but to love them is a blessing
Phases
Right now you think you're worthless
Trust me
Everybody in this world has a purpose
Phases

Promise

Mama please
Don't worry about me
There's still some things
That I got left to do

Mama dear
Don't cry don't fear
I may be troubled
But I promise to stay here

Daddy please
Don't guilt me
You won't lose another daughter
This is temporary

Like a cold front in June
Or the rain on my shoes
This won't last forever
Promise I'll make it better
I promise to get better
Promise it all gets better

Mama please
Stop calling me
If you heard me
How I sound right now
We'd both be bawling

Mama dear
I'm everything you feared
But I tried my best to make it
I swear I did

Daddy please
Come get me
I'm ready to admit
That I need help
Just give me some time
Maybe one last glass of wine

Promise I'll make it better
Promise it all gets better
I promise to get better

Mama please
Don't give up on me
Even when I pull away from you
I wish that you'd hold me

Mama dear
Don't cry don't fear
I know I'm troubled
But I promise to stay here

Bambi 22

Little Bambi
Had her life planned out
Go to school
Get 2 degrees
Move to LA by 23
Then leave the country
Work for Vice
Be a wife
Have two kids by 35

Little did she know
That's all a pipe dream
You could see in her eyes
The naivety

All she wanted
Was success and a career
She could be proud of
She loved her parents
But wanted to be
Nothing like them
She wanted passion
And adventure
Wanted freedom
But life chained her
To this dirt bag named
Restriction

Little Bambi got her heart broke quick
This bitch, Reality, kicked everything in
Little Bambi's losing all her wind
Dropping all the things
She thought she wanted

So scared of dying
She shutdown and stopped living
So scared of herself
Home girl up and went missing

Bambi's terrified
Slowly losing mind
All alone in her corner Cinderella like

Little Bambi just turned 22
Her plans are nixed
Her mind is shot
Body's damn near begun to rot
Lost all direction
Losing faith
Where's the girl
Who knew her way

Feels like a millennium
Since I've seen her
Goes MIA when reality hurts

The stress is heavily affecting her mental
Who knew anxiety was actually lethal
And now she's too risky to medicate
Too in love with the way
Prescription heroine
Makes all her troubles fade away

Some College

Some college under your belt
You tried to pass but you failed
They're looking at you so cold
You lack the smarts and they know
Some college under your belt
Some college under your belt

Better get your ass in shape
The only moolah you'll make
Is from them poles in the streets
No need for Uni degrees
Could be an entrepreneur
But you lack drive and influence
Should've stayed your ass
In school
Don't you know
Don't you know

They preach that school is so cool
And that them drugs be for fools
I'm confused
Last I checked
I was a fool but I'm cool
I got it all figured out
I got a plan and some clout
What you got
A piece of paper and doubt
Wow

She got her Uni degree
Studying psychology
So she be judging hardcore
Yet got a job doing porn
Cus no one's hiring someone
With 0 experience
Don't you know
Don't you know

So she's interning for free
And struggling just to eat
Was it worth it
Thousands in debt
Over that college degree

Oh say you can see
Bought the American dream
That shit is so over priced
We'll be in debt all our lives
Some college under my belt
A bachelors under their belt
A masters under their belt
A doctors under their belt

Some college under my belt
I tried to pass but I failed
They're looking at me so cold
They think I'm dumb but I know
I got it all figured out
Though somedays
I have my doubts
Some college under my belt
Got knowledge under my belt

34

83
Hours

83 hours sleepless
Resisting the urge
To pop a pill right now
I'm detoxing
My way off my hit list
Doctors warned me
Benzos were addictive
Took them day by day
As needed
But it wasn't enough
So I self medicated
Temporarily make
Myself go away
Drifting away
To a space in my head
Where my peace lay
Dying
Sorry but I give up on trying
Even my support system
Has me messed up
The medication and therapy
Won't help you they said
Depression ain't real
Your anxiety's fictional
It's all in your head

Mind over matter
Get that through your head
Well those that matter
Don't mind
Is my mind set
So never mind my bad habits
And the warning signs
Like the painkillers missing
And the bottles running dry
Thinking if I come home
You can help and I'll get better
But I agreed to come home
Because I knew better
There's a lot going on
I don't blame you
I've just never known
A band-aide
To heal a mental wound

April 26, 2017

I miss it so much I could cry. I want to weep, I've tried to weep but I just can't. Tears crowd the back of my throat and trickle down to the tip of my tongue. Like trying to uncover a fuzzy memory, there but not quite.

I wouldn't wish horrors on anyone be them minor or tenfold but this particular brand of awful happens to be my sliver of heaven pie. Just once, I wish you could feel what I'm talking about. Taste the danger of bliss-filled peace. Because it's worth it. Because I want you to understand my actions and how I got here.

I desperately need/want a refill of Klonopin. I don't use it the way I'm supposed to but every common disorder is unique to the individual. Everyone heals in their own way. My way of healing just happens to be a legal high prescribed by my doctor.

You see, when you take a pill from the Benzo family, it turns your world right side up. You'll know it's kicking in when the base of your neck starts to tingle and your head gets... cloudy. Not confused or dizzy, just light. You feel weightless but you struggle to keep your head up so you lie down. Then slowly, inch by inch, from head to toes, your body starts to hum a tune only you can hear. You can barely move and why would you want to. Your limbs feel strangely heavy yet you would swear you were floating. Gravity has a different effect in the land you've dosed yourself to.

I miss that feeling; short lived as it was. I miss the level of quiet my mind would achieve. The entire world silenced. Just myself and God in a cloud communicating through unspoken thoughts. All while reveling in a loving wash of warmth enveloping my body right before the smite. The lightning strike to my system jolting me off my medically induced cloud.

Grounding

Turn down the lights
Bring the quiet back
Cry Baby why don't you

Strip till you're bare
Lay down get some rest
Pray when you wake it's all over

Open the blinds
Let the sun come in
Make an effort why won't you

Paint on a smile
Make yourself believe
The reign of angst is soon over

You presume you're coming unglued
That all they see is what they get
You always have something to prove
That's a fatal lonesome circumstance

Focus
Tell me what you see around you
Reach out
For something you can feel
Eyes shut
Listen to the sound of my voice
Breath deep
Smell the sweet perfume on your skin
Now come back
Describe the taste of your lips

Up Tempo

It's one of those nights again
I'm feeling lonely and
I rather be out mind
Than sober and left behind

Give anything to force it all away
No fear no pain no more
Got the love if you've got the cure

Searching for a new found high
Something to pass away the time
Something to bring the night to life
Make me feel young and wild like

I can get up tempo to a sad song
Sway my hips to the beat of my problems
I can get up tempo to a sad song
Convince myself that worriment don't last long
Take a breath
Cry it out
And push through
In the mist of the panic
Who's got you
It's ok to get up tempo
To a sad song
Remind myself
I'm stronger in
The long run

Then & Now

I buy weed in bulk
5-10 grams at a time
That should last me
A couple weeks
If I pace myself

I bought weed in bulk
Now I have 2 grams
Sitting in a jewelry box
It's been there for
Three months

I drink a bottle of wine a day
That's the equivalent
Of one beer
I drink it through out the day
Finish it by the time
I get home
And end my evenings
With a hardier liquor

I drank a bottle of wine a day
Now I have several
Semi and full bottles
Strategically placed
Through my house
Silently comforting me with
The knowledge they're there

I sleep around
I hook up with strangers
And friends and their friends
It makes me feel wanted

I used to sleep around
The last time I had sex
Was a lot like my first
Which is probably why I don't
Sleep around the way
I used too
I don't care
To be reminded that
I'll never be good enough
When everything I am
Body, mind, heart, and soul
Are on the bed

I know not
Why I do these things
I know exactly
Why I did these things
In world terms I suffer from
Depression, anxiety and
Severe panic disorder
In my terms
I hate me a little too much

I hated me a little to much

I'm slowly making progress

Wisest of Women

After high school
Everyone had to change
To some it was easy
While others messed up everything

Maybe you don't belong
Maybe you should just go home
Give up on your hopes and dreams

But I know you can go all the way
Don't listen to what haters have to say
You will suffer and you will struggle
But your reward will be double

And I believe when all is through
You'll be the wisest of women
Because you once played the fool

Phases

Somewhere along my broken path
I took a turn and got lost
I would say things went left
But sometimes right equates to wrong
It felt right what I was doing
Got caught up in the moment
No thought on my mind
Of how it would affect me in the long term
It was good at the start
I had all the right intentions in my heart
But I took my eye off the prize
So God allowed for all of this
Hurt and confusion in my life
And I thank Him everyday
Because it forced me to wake up and realize

One
My body is a temple
I do not need a man to validate me
I am beautiful

Two
Blood may be thicker than water
But we need both to survive
And not one of them is guaranteed to you
Don't take them for granted
Don't leave them stranded
Think twice
Before you do something stupid
And take advantage

Three
My journey is my own
I will not compare the way my life is going
To where others may go

And just know
God makes everything beautiful in its time
I'm a diamond in the ruff
So I'm not really lost
I'm just in waiting to shine
There's still times
I'm pissed off about my circumstances
Still times I can't quite comprehend
All the misery I've been handed
But I know
These trials and tribulations
Are not some cruel haze
They're knowledgeable lessons
Prepping me for my fate

Phases

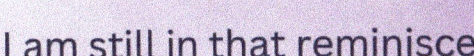

I am still in that reminisce

Then it starts to make me sad and piss me off phase

One day I pray I get to that

All happy reminders place

But

You know how it goes

My mood shifts up and down

When change hits

People come and go

We align in different stages

It's just

Phases

The Love We Deserve

Dear Wallflower,

I hope you never play the game,
"They love me, They love me not"

I hope you never waste good rain water
on beguiling Forget Me Nots

And though I cannot protect you
from the sting of acid rain

I hope it doesn't leave you so bitter
you never thirst for water again

When winter comes around
And the garden appears barren

I do hope you remember
There's a seed for every season

So when those who fed you summer squash
Disappear in the fall

There'll be plum and fig and cherry seeds
And you'll know how to grow them all

I hope you know that roses
come in different sizes shapes and colors

Each represents a type of love
In doubt seek out yellow over others

Therapy Session #1

Your intake form says you're struggling with panic attacks. How long has that been going on? Have you dealt with anxiety in previous years?

Ummm, I don't know, the past year's been really hard but this semester everything's just kind of crashing.

How are your classes going right now?

sarcastic laughter

Things are great. My hands are either shaking uncontrollably or cramping so bad I can't hold a pencil for very long. Not ideal for an art student. I suck at math. In fact I had an Algebra test yesterday. One moment I was being handed a test and the next I blacked out. And when I came too I was crying to myself in the back of the class and looked down at my test to see it was blank and time was up. Soooo ya. I'm doing GREAT.

And what about other areas of your life? How do you destress outside of school?

This is college. I go bar hopping and to random house parties. I go on Tinder and OKcupid and meet people. I doom scroll through YikYak. Just basic stuff.

How often are you drinking and doing other drugs?

looks away

You can't get in trouble for anything you say here. It's all confidential.

I don't know. I just kind of sip through out the day. It helps with the nerves. And maybe I smoke here or there at parties or kickbacks. It's not a big deal.

And when did the drinking start?

High school. Sophomore year.

Were you feeling particularly stressed back then? What was school and home life like?

Ummm, I guess I was kind of hard myself. I mean I'm not from a fancy rich family so getting into college meant I needed to work extra hard. I tried to be involved in everything I could. Guess you could say I was bit of an overachiever. Being involved so much also meant I got to stay out of the house.

Not that my family was horrible or anything. I mean I think we were pretty normal. Mom was pregnant that year so I wanted to be home even less so I wouldn't be in the path of her hormonal rage.

I started "dating" that year. That was... interesting.

After that my little sis came along. My mom and step dad were fighting a lot. Signed up for more stuff so I didn't have to hear that too. Guess I just wanted to be successful enough to have a nice quite house to myself with no drama.

Meanwhile, one of my brothers from my dad's second marriage almost died and was in and out of the hospital a lot. They live in another city so not being able to see them during those times unless it was like a "say goodbye just in case" scenario kind of sucked. I already have a complex from my little sister, his twin, dying when I was 11, but that's a story for another day.

Umm... ya. I guess with both my parents remarrying I also felt stressed to be a good big sister. All of a sudden I went form being an only child to being the oldest of eight siblings. On top of that I'm like the oldest daughter of the oldest daughter of the oldest daughter and that's like a whole thing in itself.

I don't know, I guess I just wanted to be the picture perfect student so I would be a good example. But obviously no one's perfect so I just indulged in certain things to take the edge off. A system that's been working.... until recently.

What's changed recently?

Aside from my body not wanting to be healthy and function properly. My parents appear to be on the brink of divorce and my siblings call me on the phone when they hear them fighting. It's like they think I should have all the answers and I don't know what to do from here. And even if I was with them I still wouldn't know what to do.

My grades are slipping because, again, I can't function. My love life is also kind of messy but we can shove that under a rug.

I just want to be able to go to class and live my life without having a break down every 10 minutes.

We have a lot to unpack in our next session but, for now I want to focus on getting you stable. That means going to AA meetings. Here's a pamphlet with more info. They meet on the 4th floor every Tuesday. I'm also going to prescribe you something to help with the panic attacks. You'll take it daily for the next week and then we'll see how you feel.

I don't think I need AA. I'm not an alcoholic.

You start drinking at 7 am and don't stop till you go to bed. In previous years you may have gotten away with it because you were a high functioning alcoholic, but an alcoholic none the less. And if you don't at least make an effort to get sober and healthy, I will not treat you anymore.

stares in disbelief... takes the paphlet.

Coming of Age

It felt natural
to grow like plain yellow cake batter
being poured into the center
of a cold square pan
too small for its potential

Once confined in a safe zone
I never bothered to turn the oven on
I never rose or spilled over

I am disciplined

I am

Fearful

Shrinking is a Learned Behavior

I remember when I was a child in day care
being picked up by my mother
Although they knew who she was
they would always stop her and make her prove
she was my mother
Every time

I never understood

One day when I was in kindergarten
my grandfather picked me up from latchkey
The next day the kids in my class spoke to me in Spanish
I had to explain "no habla Espanol"

They looked at me like I was loca

When I was seven
I asked my parents if I was adopted
because my skin did not match either of them
My mother a beautiful chocolate mocha
My father white-ish in pigment but not in culture

What am I?

"You are the beautiful combination of us both,"
my mother said
A light caramel, dulce de leche
Black and Mexican
Blaxican

From that day
when people asked me what I was
I'd proudly say
I'm human!
But I'm also mixed
My house has the best food

As I grew older
I began to notice more and more the rift
between my two cultures
and the hatred for people specifically like me

This is when I started shrinking

When I started the 6th grade at Cullen middle school
I attempted to make a friend out of everyone but they were
divided into cliques that determined I was neither
Mexican or Black enough to join either of them

I am still struggling to find the balance

When I was 13
starting 8th grade at a new school
I was sitting in English class when the
2 other girls in my reading group said to me
"Mixed people are so ugly... no offense."

Years later this memory is burning fresh in my mind
as though it were engraved yesterday
Nothing like being made ashamed of what you are
to make you question who you are
and shrink further and further
out of sight, out of mind, out of self

A wallflower

When I grow
Into a high functioning adult
And start making a home for me and mine
I want my future children to feel
Like they live in a house made of
Playdoh bricks

A place that sends the message:
"I am a tall sturdy oak.
Throw all of your teen angst,
Emotional trauma, puberty,
And all the B.S. life has to offer at me.
Huff all you want.
I will never falter down to rubble."

A place flexible enough
To remold itself according to their needs:
"Do you need an ear to listen, a hand to hold?
Would you prefer to vent or go over solutions?
Do you need space?"

A place that's understanding enough
To not judge during the phases of finding themselves:
"What's your vibe today?
Western, bohemian?
What's your dream?
Youtuber, doctor, fashionista, world traveler?
I can help with that."

I never want them to wonder:
"Am I loved?
Am I enough?"

I don't want them to waste time
Seeking my attention in all the wrong places

I will let them know that I am human
And sometimes I hurt too
I may cry, and take time to heal
But I will always have space for them

They do not have to walk on eggshells

Therapy Session #2

So you're going home. That's not a bad thing. You can take a semester off and get the mental and physical rest you need. Comeback in a semester or two. We can even work on getting this last semester expunged from your student record, given the circumstances.

Going home feels like giving up or like I've just failed at everything. How am I supposed to bounce back from this. I feel like everyone just handles me with kid gloves now. Like they're afraid I'm going to explode and lose my marbles at any moment.

And how does that make you feel? have you talked to them about it?

I feel like a fucking lunatic! I'm frustrated. I want everyone to just act normal. But instead they're hiding liquor bottles from me, and giving me lectures about not killing myself. My brain may be a little broken but I'm not suicidal. Jesus!

You may not be suicidal but your actions and behaviors recently could lead you to be harmed. Your friends and family just want to make sure you're safe and don't accidentally find yourself in a situation you really can't bounce back from.

I know…. I know. And I appreciate them for it. I really do. And honestly I wonder why they even still put up with me at this point.

Like the friend who drove me here and is waiting for me outside. He, out of everyone in my life right now, probably has the most valid reasons to walk away and hate me forever but he's still here.

And my roommates. God. Everyone's dealing with their own shit. I shouldn't be adding to their plate.

It's ok to lean on others sometimes. And you have an unhealthy habit of bottling everything and biting your tongue when you need help. That's partially why things have gotten this bad for you. You, need to process your emotions and speak on them as they occur, in a healthy way. Stop holding back out of fear everyone will leave you.

If someone's not positively adding to your lifestyle then why keep them around?

You wouldn't say that about someone you love if they were having a hard time so why are you saying that about yourself. Your worth is not dependent on how useful you are to someone.

shrugs uncomfortably

Let's dive deeper into the topic of self worth for a moment because it's bleeding into other areas of your life as well. You mentioned previously that you were "talking" to someone and falling for them but you didn't feel worthy of them.

Why is that?

rolls eyes

You don't think very highly of yourself. You have a tendency to equate your worth in romantic relationships to whether or not someone desires you.

Ha! Then I must not be worth very much. I'm not exactly the average persons cup of tea. Crazy or not.

You know, you can continue putting extreme amounts of pressure on yourself. You can continue stretching yourself thin and neglecting your own needs to feel needed. You can even continue having sex with strangers to fill that void of self loathing, but you're only going to make things worse for yourself.

slowly shakes head in angry denial

You've already expressed that sex without emotion makes you feel more depressed. Yet you continue to throw yourself at these people who want nothing more then your body for the sake of feeling beautiful and desired, worthy. You say it's a distraction from the pressure you feel, a lot of which you're putting your self under, but it seems to be a two birds one stone kind of thing.

It all circles back to self worth for you. The drinking, the smoking, the sleeping around, the depression, the panic disorder.

You are worthy of love. You are worthy simply because you exist. You deserve to be loved; not because you do a service for someone, not because you give them more of you then you should; but because you simply exist.

stares blankly and teary eyed

deep sigh

How's your medication. Any changes?

Mmmm. I still feel the same. The panic attacks haven't stopped. They're getting worse.

You can stop taking that prescription. It was just a placebo. Here, fill this out at the student pharmacy. We'll check back in 2 weeks and after that, in one month. Student still or not, we'll continue working through this together.

You're young
The goal shouldn't be to love someone
That doesn't mean you have to stay alone
I know it's hard
I know it's confusing
Mom and dad gave you examples not worth using
So you run away
From mistakes they made
Even though there's no one there to run from

Deep down you know that's not alright
Sometimes love requires a fight or flight response
Maybe you should fight for once

I know
Children of divorce
Don't always end up loving the "right way"
I know
Because I've let a thing or two get in my way

You're older now
And all your friends are "talking" now
You're starting to get desperate now
So you invite every stranger home
Till one sticks around, knocks you down
Or cheats on you
That's not love
But it's acceptable to you

You know deep down that isn't right
Sometimes love requires a fight or flight response
You need to learn the difference

I know
Children of divorce
Don't always end up loving the right way
I know
Because a thing or two has left me in disarray

Children of Divorce

When You Say You Love Me

I don't believe you when you say you love me
I don't believe you when you say you care
That crooked smile and the redness in your eyes
Lets me know your body's here
But your heart is elsewhere

I can feel it in the way you won't hold me
I can feel it when you kiss my neck
Avoid my lips because that's too intimate
And I fall easily so we can't go there

I do believe you when you say you need me
I see it in your eyes you're down and low
Well I know I'm not what or who you want
But I promise to love you right
If it makes YOU feel a little less alone

I want to believe you when you say you love ME

Casual Affairs

Can you scent that in the air
(*sniff* aah)
Someone just found release
Nigga I was there
"Word?"
It just wasn't me
"Damn!"
It's almost never me
With casual comes
Casualties

Bless my soul
I'm in desperate need of
Self control

I cannot lust on like this
A junkie feening an
Orgasmic fix
Searching for love
Where love don't exist
A game of lust and politics

Called
Casual affairs
Neither here nor there
Night owls beware
Of casual affairs

I like how we keep things casual
You like it when I do you dirty
I like how we say this is casual
But the next day
We're both running
Back into each others arms
Claiming we're just bored

So we post up
Playing house
All about each other
But it's still casual
He's sure

I like it when he
Hits it from behind
Because I can't gaze in his eyes
And see the absence of love
Or someone I don't trust
It's lust and pixie dust

Casual affairs
They happen everywhere
Day and night beware
Of casual affairs

Novocain

1

I am just a toy
You like to call up on the weekends
You're just a drug
A substitution for my feelings
Take another hit of that tree
Nigga don't torch my weed
Tincture straight to the brain
Make my heart pump
Novocain

2

No one knows me the way You do
It's too bad
We're both ignorant to truth
Of what this is and why we return to it often
Your heart beats to fast to fall in sync
And mines too numb to know love is an option

3

Maybe that's why I love him
Maybe that's why we hate me
Maybe that's why I'm failing
That's probably why I'll forever be a play thing

4

Listen...
You're just a toy
I like to indulge on the weekends
Because I need a drug
A substitution for my feelings
I just want to be on my own
Without feeling alone
So take a hit
Take a shot
Do a drop
Get out our minds
Do something wrong

5

Make me
Forget that I'm alone
Forget that I'm not strong
Forget who in the spirit I am
I hate who I am

6

Call me out my name
Call me a bitch
Call me insane

7

Strip me bare
Be my distraction
Try not to care
There's no attachments

8

I am just a toy
I'm played with weekend to weekend
There really is no drug
That could substitute my feelings
Take another hit of that tree
Damn somebody torched my weed
Flip a switch in my brain
Make my heart pump
Novocain

Nostalgia

Swisher Sweet clouding up the memory
Swisher Swisher baby so sweet
Leave me here
I like dreaming
Leave me here
I still believe in you

Nostalgia
Got me messed up got me just right
Nostalgia
Looks like nudity under the moonlight
Nostalgia
Taste like fresh green rolled in blue berries
Taste like the best lips to have ever graced mine
Like finding comfort in your arms while the stars shine
The scent of dove soap the feel of soft skin
The butterflies in my stomach from never knowing
The situation
Were we more than just friends
Darling them was the days
Baby that was a time
Check your watch
Forever frozen at a quarter past live

And now this Swisher Sweet is clouding up the memory
Swisher Swisher baby too sweet
Leave me here
I like dreaming
Leave me here
When I believed in you

Nostalgia
Got me messed up this buzz is finite
Nostalgia
Quick roll another one inhale and ignite
Nostalgia
Sound like Lemonade over ice
Mixed with sweet and sour you're a hint of naughty and nice
Doing me all kinds of good up in the bedroom
So good I forget the insecurities you worsen with the things you do

But
Sugar them was the days
Baby that was a time
Check your watch
Forever frozen at three quarters past live

So I smoke Swisher Sweets to cloud up all my memories
Swisher Swisher baby too sweet
Leave me here
I like dreaming
Leave me here
My beliefs changed in you

The W's

Where do you go
What do you do
When it's 2 a.m. and the city's
Closing down on you

When your house ain't a home
And there's no one around
To keep you from crashing
All the way down
To the ground

Wish you would stay
a bit longer
Take hold of my hand
As long as we're together
This night never has to end

And
I don't wanna be alone tonight
I don't wanna risk
losing the fight
The war that's brewing
in my mind

So
What do you do
Where do you go
When you look around
And suddenly you're all alone

When everyone
has their own thing
And you get lost in the mix
And you keep hoping somehow
Someday you'll get used to this

Get used to dancing the lonely
Get used to singing the blues
Get used to everyone you love
Saying goodbye to you

I can't bare to be alone tonight
I have finite strength left to fight
The war I'm losing in my mind

Who do you turn to
Who do you call
When life is upside down
And you can't figure
Right from wrong

Why do I cry in silence
Why don't I ask for help
Why am I built this way
Why do I self deprecate
Say I'm lonely then isolate

I really shouldn't
be alone tonight
I've exhausted
all my ways to fight
The unending war
decimating my mind

Help me silence the empty void
Scream l love you at the top of
your lungs
Hold me till l can feel
how I am enough
I need someone to
speak louder
Than the dark in the ruff

Help me not
disappear to the void
Love me despite
all the wrong that I've done
Hold me like an answer that you'll
never give up
Love me louder
than I myself ever could

Therapy Session #3

It's been five years since you've dated or "talked" to someone. It's natural to be nervous.

I don't even know where to start. Like how to strike up a conversation, or even flirt. It already feels like too much and I want to say let's just try again next year.

Ha, Well you could continue putting it off but last session you were determined to at least try to put yourself out there again. And as for conversation starters, the apps have those now to help get things flowing. As for flirting, you give a little smile, toss the hair, do the lock eyes and look away move. Heck, you can even watch tutorials on Youtube of how to flirt.

So what else is holding you back?

It's the pictures. I look like a fuggly rag doll in all my photos. Plus most of them are old, my bodies changed.

Are you happy with your body now?

I've lost 70 pounds but I still look like a pale oompa loompa. And an extra jiggly one at that. The weight loss just made everything saggy and I feel so uncomfortable because I'm not used to maneuvering in my body as it is now.

That's understandable. You've had major health changes over the past year. It takes time to adjust. However; that's not an excuse to bad talk yourself.

I'm giving you a home work assignment. Till our next appointment I want you to look in the mirror for 5 minutes a day and compliment yourself. List things you like about yourself. Touch your body and get comfortable with it. Tell yourself how beautiful you are, because you are.

Mmmm. *rolls eyes*

When was the last time you felt beautiful?

shakes head and shifts uncomfortably.

I don't remember. I mean I don't think I'm like the most hideous thing in the world, I just... I don't know!

Ok but, do You FEEL beautiful right now?

In a way I guess so. But I really don't like that word. It doesn't sit right with me.

And why is that?

Well.... I.... It... I feel like I'm not beautiful... "enough."

Can you elaborate?

Growing up. When boys started noticing me it was always in a flirty way that got more sexual as I got older. And more... aggressive I guess you could say.

And sometimes that felt nice. The flirty part, flirting was fun. Becoming sexually awakened was fun.

But one day I realized there was no in between with boys. I was either a sexual object to be used and tossed aside or I was the girl they saw as a sister figure. Forever friend zoned.

And sometimes that was nice. The knowing where I stood part. And friends are good. Friends are safe, mostly.

But I would look at other girls with their boyfriends and wonder how I could be that kind of girl. Not just the too sexy or too ugly girl. But the loving girl.

And then you know life happened. The boys got even more aggressive. More sneaky. More cunning and I...

Well that's when the incident happened...

I spiraled. Emotionally, mentally, physically. Lost myself, found myself. That seems to be a never ending process. Rather annoying actually.

And after everything that's happened then and even up to now, I've come to realize that I just really. REALLY Hate. When people call me beautiful.

Because every time they do it just reminds me... *tries real hard not to cry*

Reminds you that you were raped?

flinches and looks away

You know you can't keep calling it an "incident that made you uncomfortable." You. Were. Raped. You told that man NO countless times as he followed you and proceeded to take advantage of you.

It was years ago and besides, it's not like it was violent... I didn't scream, or try to run when he... I froze. I sat there and cried like a deer in headlights.

That's still rape. And if you can't admit that to yourself you will never be able to actually process it and heal...

stares at each other in silence

He kept saying it while it was happening.

Saying what?

"You're beautiful. You're beautiful.
I just wanna fuck you, you're so beautiful."

So hearing someone call you beautiful is triggering.

I hate when people call me beautiful because hearing that just reminds me that I'm beautiful enough to rape, but not beautiful enough to actually be loved.

And that's really fucking depressing.

In His Eyes

I let him touch me one last time
Looked at each other with no love in our eyes
Well I know what this is and who you are
And after years we're just now getting this far

When you get the angle right let go of my hand
Don't start acting different when the night ends
If you see me around don't look the other way
No matter how I try you'll never be a stranger babe

Because for years this is how I've recognized you
By this glazed over "piece of ass" look in your eyes
And for years I foolishly believed
I was nothing more than how you looked at me

I think about why I let him in
He set the tone for all my men
There's something missing but I can't quite place it
Whore in the making and I always faked it

One tried to treat me right and held me tighter
One pointed out that I was afraid of desire
But when I looked at them all I saw was you
Different eyes
Same old issue

For years this is how I've recognized you
By that glazed over "pleasure toy" look in your eyes
And for years I whole heartedly believed
That I was nothing more than how you looked at me

I go out every now and then
Playing games I shouldn't wanna win
There's validation in the sense that they want me
But in the end I feel disgusted and guilty

One called me beautiful and then he touched me
I sat there crying
Deer in headlights while he ***** me
He never called again but I don't really care
You're in the eyes of every liar out there

For years this is how I've recognized you
By this glazed over "she deserves this" look in your eyes
And for years I was determined to believe
That I was nothing more than how you looked at me

I look back on those nights so embarrassed
It breaks my heart so say that's my life and it happened
Now when I think of them I feel so ashamed

As each one walked away He left me with myself to blame

There's Something Wrong

I'll admit
I have never been in a serious relationship
No one to call bae
No one to see on a regular basis
And I can't explain why
Honest I've tried
Lord knows I've tried

There's something wrong with me
I've been serial dating
And yet I'm still lonely
There must be something wrong with me

My generation doesn't understand
That true love doesn't stem from one night stands
They all want to "talk" but only through text
We want to get intimate
While never knowing the person
We're afraid of getting close
Because our parents proved
We'll only end up alone

There's something wrong with us
We've been so ironically out of touch
That we forgot how to trust
I know there's something wrong with us

I accept people who treat me like shit
So at the end of the night
There's someone sharing my bed
It leaves me empty and sad
If people accept the love
They think they deserve
I don't know what I've done
To deserve this level of hurt

There's something wrong with me
I've been constantly shagging
Trying to cure my lonely
I know there's something wrong with me

Teach Me

Teach me
How to body this house
Inhabit this mouth
This skin
These feet
These limbs

Teach me
How to body this house
A pre manufactured shell
with default settings
That you expected me to
override and manually change
With no access code
No directions
No tools
No help

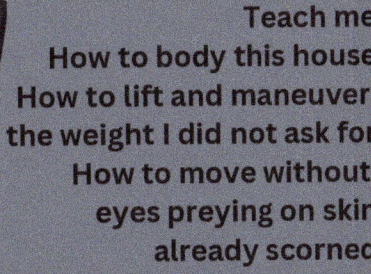

Teach me
How to body this house
How to lift and maneuver
the weight I did not ask for
How to move without
eyes preying on skin
already scorned

Teach me
How to be a woman
How to move my hips
How to smack my lips
How to be attractive
without offending the
masses

Teach me
How to body this house

Therapy Session #4

So how's the past month been for you?

Good. A lot, but good. I'm still adjusting to living on my own but I think it was the best move for everyone.

Agreed. You needed your own space to be independent of your family. And there may be some growing pains but ultimately you will be OK. Your mom and your sister will be OK.

And how have you been spending your time?

Mainly just working from home. Honestly I haven't left my apartment in 6 weeks now.

Like at all?

Nope. Not to check the mail, grocery shopping, a walk, nada.

Ma'am that is not ok. Why aren't we leaving the house?

I don't know what to do with myself. Also my work schedule isn't really set up to have a social life on a regular. Plus I have like 3 friends and only one lives in town. And I feel like if I keep reaching out to her then I'm like bothering her which is stupid because she's my best friend, but the anxious voice in my head is telling me to stop bothering people and be alone.

Ok so I'm hearing we need to set up some work boundaries and make a game plan to socialize more. So homework assignment. Put in a schedule request for certain hours. Even if it can't be a normal 9-5 or weekends off, at least a designated time every week that allows you to plan something that day.

Next, make a list of things you can do around your city, whether it's by yourself or with a friend, and this week pick at least 1 thing on that list to do.

Next, make a new friend. Yes you may have your group but when your group is spread out or you have different schedules you need other people to hang out with. Maybe you can try joining a club of some sort.

Ok that seems like a lot and I already want to cry.

You're going to be fine. I promise.

Mmmmm.

It's this or sit alone in your apartment for another 6 weeks. That's not healthy and I do not want to have to call the police to do a wellness check on you. Get out of the house.

I know. I know but I don't... I feel extra lonely now that it's just me all the time and I don't want to be lonely but I don't want to be a bother, or be codependent in an unhealthy way anymore either.

Like, now I'm not the first call if my mom needs something or if my sister needs something. I feel like I just lost a child a little bit because the way we were set up was like being a work from home mom. And now there's no one there to mother and I have to go be single and independent, which I technically always was, but now my life is set up to actually live that way and that's hard to face.

I used my family as an excuse not to put myself out there anymore.

Without any excuses, where do I hide? My new apartment, that's where. Heck I'm paying for it, I might as well enjoy it.

It's ok to have an adjustment period. It's a big adjustment! It's ok to enjoy your new apartment. You made a big change and accomplished an important milestone.

HOWEVER, it's not ok to sit at home as much as you do to the point that nice new apartment is more jail cell than home. You live there, you work there, you need some kind of balance or you're going to go stir crazy.

So yes. Leave the house and go make friends. Start dating again. Find new hobbies. You have a whole life to live so go live it!

Sunshine

A peculiar thing,
in all my years chasing star dust I never thought:
What comes next?

Never stoped to smell the roses in bloom
or stuck around long enough to care what the Sun might have to
offer.

As the Sun rose over the horizon
I was befuddled at the water color picture before me.

"You're beautiful!,"
I shouted;
no longer afraid of what the clouds may think.

"So are you!,"
he replied;
keeping distance so not to burn me.

I knew then that this too was love.

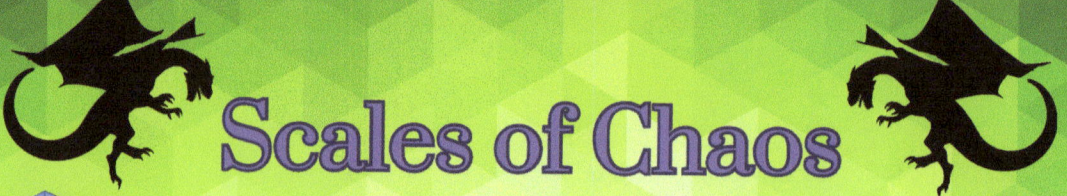

Scales of Chaos

I went into a dragons lair and came out like a bad ass
I fought
I healed
I almost died
I took a long rest and was fully revived

I made enemies I made friends
I found framily in the process
We formed a party of traumatized women
I'm the King and Umiko's the make a wish princess

I talk to the moon and Cherry to the stars
Crystal grows "herbs" and Hypatia is bougie
Zyxzera's magic is sometimes scary cus tentacles
But our favorite Dungeon Master finds it amusing

I have always grappled with chaos
But never quite like this
I'd like to thank each party member
For giving me this gift

From session zero to a two year campaign
Still leveling up and going strong
Here's to nat 20s and Inspiration
And many years to come

Wherever our solo adventures take us
I want everyone to know
You were all worth leaving the house for
And I'll carry you with me wherever I go

- Love, Your High King
Bambi

Friends from College

To Thing 1, Thing 2, and Mz. Frizzle:

Thank you,
For the nights we won't remember
With people we'll never forget.
Thank you,
For showing me more to life
Then my anxiety ever did.
Thank you,
For not giving up on me
When I was at my worst.
Thank you,
For always showing up,
In good times and in bad.
Thank you,
For teaching me that friendship
Stretches farther then 20 miles.
Thank you,
For keeping me safe
When I couldn't protect myself.
Thank you,
For pushing me outside my comfort zone
And helping me to grow.
Thank you,
For believing in me
When I didn't believe in myself.
Thank you,
For the joy,
For the laughter,
For the hugs,
For the love.
Thank you,
For being my friend.

(PS. you're never getting rid of me - Love Chelsea)

Mother

I am a Wallflower
So are you
I failed to see it before
but now I do

I used to think you were a field daisy
Wild and care free
Blowing wherever the wind
Whispered you needed to be

My mother the 20 something
My mother the party girl
My mother the adventuress
My mother the Black Superwoman

But

I was a child
I didn't know any better
I didn't realize you were struggling
Or see the storms that you weathered

Mother I am a wall flower
And for a time you were too
I didn't always understand this
But now that I do

You are more than a field daisy
You're a field of flowers in bloom
And as the seasons change
So too do you

My mother the angry black woman
My mother the broken hearted
My mother the persevering
My mother the God fearing

Now

I see you
And I understand the cost
To be a strong black woman
Means sacrifice and loss

Because the world doesn't know
What to do with women like you
They are scared of your strength
And envious of your skin
So they made you a sort of wallflower
Thinking it'd prevent all your wins

But no

Mother
I won't always be a wallflower
And that's in large part thanks to you
In every storm that's past
You've never failed to see me through

And when people say
"You're just like your mother!"
I'll grin at them and recall
The legacy of a Strong Black Woman
Who outgrew
The wall

I Love _____

(Insert Name Here),
It's ok to be you unapologetically.
Not everyone will be happy,
or satisfied, or content with you.
Not everyone will understand
your choices, your vision, your power.
You are not a child.
Speak and act like a confidant adult when they question your
muchness.
You are not a saint.
Speak and act like a respectful adult
and be thankful for the ones who helped you when broken.
Be thankful for the ones who helped while broken.

(Insert Name Here),
You are not a play thing.
You are not unworthy of love or kindness.
If someone treats you like a piece of chewing gum that's lost its flavor
do not be afraid to walk away and say you deserve better.
LOVE YOURSELF!
Body your own house.
Inhale new life back into the old bones and skin
you had forsaken.
Revive yourself.
That house you body has a foundation crafted by God
specifically for you.
Your being has a destined purpose.
Walk in it.
Even if you have to start with baby steps,
walk in it.

Do this and someday the life you love will love you back.

Do this and say, "I love (Insert Name Here)."

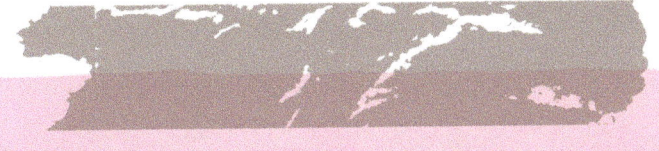

I Love _____

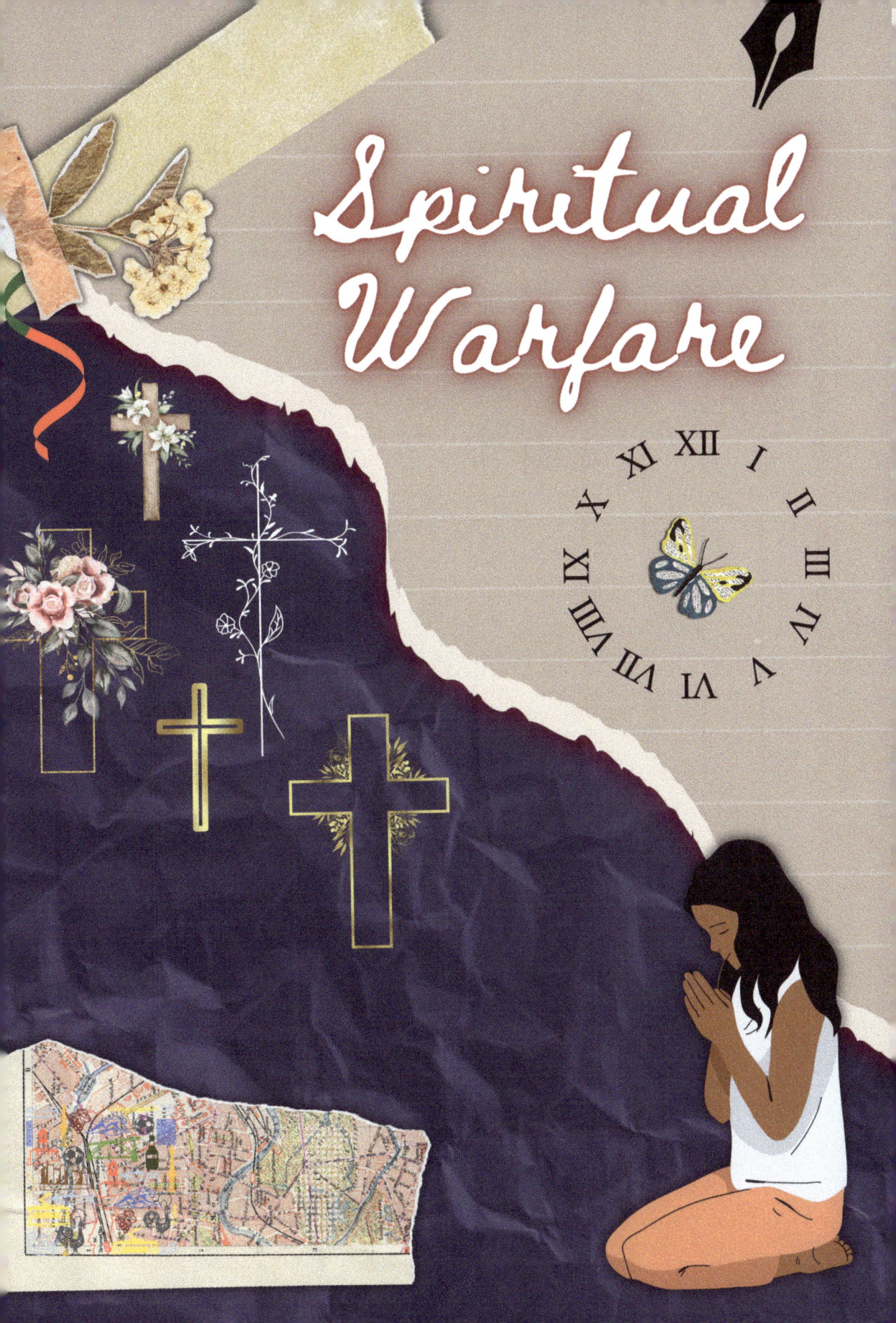

Spiritual Warfare

Dear wallflower,

I am so sorry

I thought that giving you water
Was enough to say I love you
But I realize now I didn't know
How to read the language
Your love was written in

I am trying to do better

And I know we struggle
To believe it sometimes
A lot of the time
All of the time
But You are amazing
You deserve all the sunshine
This life has to offer

Wallflower You are enough

And I know You're alone most days
So you don't hear it enough
But when no one else is there to say it
I encourage You to look Me in the mirror
And say

I love You
I LOVE You
I Love YOU

God don't let my mind be the end of me.
God don't let my mind be the end of me.
God don't let my mind be the end of me.
God don't let my mind be the end of me.
God don't let my mind be the end of me.
God don't let my mind be the end of me.
God don't let my mind be the end of me.
God don't let my mind be the end of me.
God don't let my mind be the end of me.
God don't let my mind be the end of me.
God don't let my mind be the end of me.
God don't let my mind be the end of me.
God don't let my mind be the end of me.
God don't let my mind be the end of me.
God don't let my mind be the end of me.
God don't let my mind be the end of me.
God don't let my mind be the end of me.
God don't let my mind be the end of me.
God don't let my mind be the end of me.
God don't let my mind be the end of me.
God don't let my mind be the end of me.
God don't let my mind be the end of me.
God don't let my mind be the end of me.
God don't let my mind be the end of me.
God don't let my mind be the end of me.
God don't let my mind be the end of me.
God don't let my mind be the end of me.
God don't let my mind be the end of me.
God don't let my mind be the end of me.
God don't let my mind be the end of me.
God don't let my mind be the end of me.
God don't let my mind be the end of me.
God don't let my mind be the end of me.
God don't let my mind be the end of me.
God don't let my mind be the end of me.
God don't let my mind be the end of me.
God don't let my mind be the end of me.
God don't let my mind be the end of me.
God don't let my mind be the end of me.
God don't let my mind be the end of me.
God don't let my mind be the end of me.
God don't let my mind be the end of me.
God don't let my mind be the end of me.
God don't let my mind be the end of me.
God don't let my mind be the end of me.
God don't let my mind be the end of me.
God don't let my mind be the end of me.
God don't let my mind be the end of me.
God don't let my mind be the end of me.

God don't let my mind be the end of me.
God don't let my mind be the end of me.
God don't let my mind be the end of me.
God don't let my mind be the end of me.
God don't let my mind be the end of me.
God don't let my mind be the end of me.
God don't let my mind be the end of me.
God don't let my mind be the end of me.
God don't let my mind be the end of me.
God don't let my mind be the end of me.
God don't let my mind be the end of me.
God don't let my mind be the end of me.
God don't let my mind be the end of me.
God don't let my mind be the end of me.
God don't let my mind be the end of me.
God don't let my mind be the end of me.
God don't let my mind be the end of me.
God don't let my mind be the end of me.
God don't let my mind be the end of me.
God don't let my mind be the end of me.
God don't let my mind be the end of me.
God don't let my mind be the end of me.
God don't let my mind be the end of me.
God don't let my mind be the end of me.
God don't let my mind be the end of me.
God don't let my mind be the end of me.
God don't let my mind be the end of me.
God don't let my mind be the end of me.
God don't let my mind be the end of me.
God don't let my mind be the end of me.
God don't let my mind be the end of me.
God don't let my mind be the end of me.
God don't let my mind be the end of me,
God don't let my mind be the end of me.
God don't let my mind be the end of me.
God don't let my mind be the end of me.
God don't let my mind be the end of me.
God don't let my mind be the end of me.
God don't let my mind be the end of me.
God don't let my mind be the end of me.
God don't let my mind be the end of me.
God don't let my mind be the end of me.
God don't let my mind be the end of me.
God don't let my mind be the end of me.
God don't let my mind be the end of me.

God don't let
God don't let
God don't let
God don't let
God don't let
God don't let
God don't let
God don't let
God don't let
God don't let
God don't let
God don't let
God don't let
God don't let
God don't let
God don't let
God don't let
God don't let
God don't let
God don't let
God don't let
God don't let
God don't let
God don't let
God don't let
God don't let
God don't let
God don't let
God don't let
God don't let
God don't let
God don't let
God don't let
God don't let
God don't let
God don't let
God don't let
God don't let
God don't let
God don't let
God don't let
God don't let
God don't let
God don't let

the end of me. God don't let my mind be the end of me. God don't let my mind be the end of me.
the end of me. God don't let my mind be the end of me. God don't let my mind be the end of me.
the end of me. God don't let my mind be the end of me. God don't let my mind be the end of me.
the end of me. God don't let my mind be the end of me. God don't let my mind be the end of me.
the end of me. God don't let my mind be the end of me. God don't let my mind be the end of me.
the end of me. God don't let my mind be the end of me. God don't let my mind be the end of me.
the end of me. God don't let my mind be the end of me. God don't let my mind be the end of me.
the end of me. God don't let my mind be the end of me. God don't let my mind be the end of me.
the end of me. God don't let my mind be the end of me. God don't let my mind be the end of me.
the end of me. God don't let my mind be the end of me. God don't let my mind be the end of me.
the end of me. God don't let my mind be the end of me. God don't let my mind be the end of me.
the end of me. God don't let my mind be the end of me. God don't let my mind be the end of me.
the end of me. God don't let my mind be the end of me. God don't let my mind be the end of me.
the end of me. God don't let my mind be the end of me. God don't let my mind be the end of me.
the end of me. God don't let my mind be the end of me. God don't let my mind be the end of me.
the end of me. God don't let my mind be the end of me. God don't let my mind be the end of me
the end of me. God don't let my mind be the end of me. God don't let my mind be the end of me
the end of me. God don't let my mind be the end of me. God don't let my mind be the end of me
the end of me. God don't let my mind be the end of me. God don't let my mind be the end of me
the end of me. God don't let my mind be the end of me. God don't let my mind be the end of me
the end of me. God don't let my mind be the end of me. God don't let my mind be the end of me
the end of me. God don't let my mind be the end of me. God don't let my mind be the end of me
the end of me. God don't let my mind be the end of me. God don't let my mind be the end of me
the end of me. God don't let my mind be the end of me. God don't let my mind be the end of me
the end of me. God don't let my mind be the end of me. God don't let my mind be the end of me
the end of me. God don't let my mind be the end of me. God don't let my mind be the end of me
the end of me. God don't let my mind be the end of me. God don't let my mind be the end of me
the end of me. God don't let my mind be the end of me. God don't let my mind be the end of me
the end of me. God don't let my mind be the end of me. God don't let my mind be the end of me
the end of me. God don't let my mind be the end of me. God don't let my mind be the end of me
the end of me. God don't let my mind be the end of me. God don't let my mind be the end of me
the end of me. God don't let my mind be the end of me. God don't let my mind be the end of me
the end of me. God don't let my mind be the end of me. God don't let my mind be the end of me
the end of me. God don't let my mind be the end of me. God don't let my mind be the end of me
the end of me. God don't let my mind be the end of me. God don't let my mind be the end of me
the end of me. God don't let my mind be the end of me. God don't let my mind be the end of me
the end of me. God don't let my mind be the end of me. God don't let my mind be the end of me
the end of me. God don't let my mind be the end of me. God don't let my mind be the end of me
the end of me. God don't let my mind be the end of me. God don't let my mind be the end of me
the end of me. God don't let my mind be the end of me. God don't let my mind be the end of me
the end of me. God don't let my mind be the end of me. God don't let my mind be the end of me
the end of me. God don't let my mind be the end of me. God don't let my mind be the end of me
the end of me. God don't let my mind be the end of me. God don't let my mind be the end of me
the end of me. God don't let my mind be the end of me. God don't let my mind be the end of me
the end of me. God don't let my mind be the end of me. God don't let my mind be the end of me
the end of me. God don't let my mind be the end of me. God don't let my mind be the end of me
the end of me. God don't let my mind be the end of me. God don't let my mind be the end of me
the end of me. God don't let my mind be the end of me. God don't let my mind be the end of me
the end of me. God don't let my mind be the end of me. God don't let my mind be the end of me
the end of me. God don't let my mind be the end of me. God don't let my mind be the end of me
the end of me. God don't let my mind be the end of me. God don't let my mind be the end of m
the end of me. God don't let my mind be the end of me. God don't let my mind be the end of m
the end of me. God don't let my mind be the end of me. God don't let my mind be the end of m

A Soul Worthy

Come over here
Get high
I'd give anything to feel alright
Do you believe that in His eyes
We're never gunna reach
The heavenly sky

Never will I reach
Never will I be at peace
I just want to see my Lord in the sky

Can someone carry me
Can someone show me
How to be
A soul worthy of
The heavenly sky

My vibe well ok I'll admit
There's days when I wake up and I just don't believe in it
Not sure if I'm a Christian or if I believe in Christ
Like I know that God exist but does existing make him right
You know what
It's the religion of it all that has me trippin
It's creating a cognitive dissonance
Between myself and my so called demons
If the bible is law
And y'all believe every word to be true
I question if you read your damnation
All the way through

Cus I've been
Eating with me demons
Sleeping with my demons
Praying for my demons
Praying with my demons

And you're looking at me
As though I've made no sense
Yet you're offended
So I know you understand what I'm saying
I'm calling out
All the hateful blasphemy
You've been praying
Ironic how
You've become the very thing that you hated

You need a blunt sis
Inhale the peace release the madness
Calm down
Take a hit of this
Now you ain't righteous
Trip up and pass it

In My Head

Y'all I'm not right in my head
Sometimes I swear I'm better off dead
Funny
Because death's my number one fear
At times that's the only thing keeping me here
Pop a pill for everything I feel
And everything that I don't
Pop a pill for everything I will
Take me off my meds and I won't
Live
Because I'm forever glued to my bed
These invisible chains have me stuck
These beautiful lies
Like happy in my eyes
It's all in my head and it's all mixed up

Lord take this evil off of my spirit
Have mercy on my soul
One day I pray I'm forgiven
For all the wasted time that I stole
For all the one night stands that I had
For neglecting my responsibilities
As a daughter, sister, and friend

I avoided the pressure
And all it caused me was pain
I avoided the pressure
And not a single blessing I gained
So I disappear when the week ends
Mess around get lost in the deep end
Life has no float
It keeps drowning me
And I have no desire to swim

Corpse Flower

Trying to remain sober
when hell's favorite demons
are dancing around you
is like being a
Corpse Flower
waiting to bloom.

I've been rooted and unwavering
for so long.
One petal
tightly gripped around an
outstretched tongue
in search or something more palatable
than fresh rain water.

I thirst for living water.

Recovery

When a plant is infested:

It has to be isolated from the others so the disease doesn't spread.
It has to be blasted with water to wash away the pest.
It needs to be repotted with fresh soil.
The roots may even need to be trimmed to avoid root rot.
Old flowers and leaves are removed to redirect energy to new growth.

A recovering plant needs just the right conditions to revive or you can send it into shock.
It may look good for a few days then die suddenly.
No new roots ever established, no growth, just a short lived moment of beauty at the end of its life.

But in the event it accepts its new environment it will grow strong healthy roots.

Establishing a home.

Slowly you will see new leaves, flower buds, and eventually blooms in just the right season.

Where Are You?

Where are you
Wallflower
I don't see you
in the coffee shop
working on your book
Your instrument
hasn't been touched
in weeks
The new equipment
you bought
still in boxes

Where are you
Wallflower
I see the sink is
over flowing
with dirty dishes
and ill timed
baking adventures
The trash is in
such abundance

I honestly don't know
what is and isn't
trash anymore

Where are you
Wallflower
I tried talking
to the walls
but they give nothing
away for free
Are they holding you
hostage

Where are you
Wallflower
Just let us know
you're alright
That you're alive
If you need help
we'll be right here
We can sit alone
in silence together

Mustard Seed

Lately my souls been feeling itchy
Like there isn't enough comfort to go around
Or not enough quiet to silence the lonely
Not enough calm in this body to stay still

So I swallowed a mustard seed
A herbal remedy to soothe the ache
A little symbol of faith

And not unlike a battery erupted
The acid inside me corroded that seed
Until it turned to something unrecognizable
But familiar amongst all the other trash
My dreams
My prayers

Hello Father

Hello Father
I know I've made many mistakes
I've had pleasure I've had pain
But nothing compares to You

Oh my God
Won't You please lend a hand
Or grant me access to the land
Of which I came

Hello Father
If You're listening and You care
Why won't You answer my prayer
My faith is staggering

Oh my God
Can You hear my soul on fire
Is that to punish or refine
Lord show me mercy

Hello Father
Is this what life was meant to be
Souls just drowning in a sea
Of tumultuous despair

Oh my God
Heal me at my core
Make me better then before
I fell from grace

Convos w/ God

I see you crying. I hear your pain.

So what? You want a reward for that?

Tell me why you're hurting.

Aren't You supposed to be able to read minds or auras or whatever!
You tell me!

Silence

Of course, always asking questions or talking in riddles but never really giving answers or clear explanations. I'M TIRED! I'm tired, I'm so tired! And angry! And sad.
But You know what? It doesn't matter. I'm going to wipe my face and keep pretending that everything is fine because everything is as it should be right?

This is all part of the grand design, God knows best B.S. Not that it's B.S. but it FEELS like bull shit. Run and tell THAT to Your....
What, master? Father?
Trinity bros? IDK

Silence & Tears

We are waiting....

Hysterical Laughter

that's a 3 faced answer if there ever was one.

Waiting... Soon.... In the near future... some day... when the time is right...

What if the time turns into never? If I disobeyed or fumbled the blessing then just say that! Because I'm tired of waiting, of hoping only for nothing to come of it. .

I've been clinging to that vision you showed me years ago. Telling myself "God's going to take care of it, keep pushing. God said He would do a thing and He will, keep it pushing. Don't give up, God's got you."

It's starting to feel like a lie.

Like I'm delusional for thinking God would ever show me the happy go lucky version of my future I so desperately wanted.

The land, the family, the love, the joy. The peace.

I've questioned it so much I've gone from thinking, you know what, maybe, just maybe, that vision is real but its not here. I only get to experience that when I die.

Death started to look a whole lot better despite my fear of it.

Then I thought, NO. That's not it, I must have just been such a colossal disappointment that I don't get that blessing anymore. It was a possibility but, oops oh well, now you get to be lonely, depressed, and over all just mentally F'd forever but you still gotta' live by "kingdom rules" or else.

And then death started looking even better.

And I know You saw me pick up that blade. You saw my tears, You heard my pain yet where were You???????

I was crying FOR YOU! I was praying that You would swoop down and save the day. And DO NOT say me putting down the blade after a few nicks was saving the day because the only thing that kept me from fully committing was fear of retribution.

It didn't take away the overwhelming feeling of wanting to be anywhere but here.

Heal me, change me, make me brand new God.
Heal me, change me, make me brand new God.
Heal me, change me, make me brand new God.
Heal me, change me, make me brand new God.
Heal me, change me, make me brand new God.
Heal me, change me, make me brand new God.
Heal me, change me, make me brand new God.
Heal me, change me, make me brand new God.
Heal me, change me, make me brand new God.
Heal me, change me, make me brand new God.
Heal me, change me, make me brand new God.
Heal me, change me, make me brand new God.
Heal me, change me, make me brand new God.
Heal me, change me, make me brand new God.
Heal me, change me, make me brand new God.
Heal me, change me, make me brand new God.
Heal me, change me, make me brand new God.
Heal me, change me, make me brand new God.
Heal me, change me, make me brand new God.
Heal me, change me, make me brand new God.
Heal me, change me, make me brand new God.
Heal me, change me, make me brand new God.
Heal me, change me, make me brand new God.
Heal me, change me, make me brand new God.
Heal me, change me, make me brand new God.
Heal me, change me, make me brand new God.
Heal me, change me, make me brand new God.
Heal me, change me, make me brand new God.
Heal me, change me, make me brand new God.
Heal me, change me, make me brand new God.
Heal me, change me, make me brand new God.
Heal me, change me, make me brand new God.
Heal me, change me, make me brand new God.
Heal me, change me, make me brand new God.
Heal me, change me, make me brand new God.
Heal me, change me, make me brand new God.
Heal me, change me, make me brand new God.
Heal me, change me, make me brand new God.
Heal me, change me, make me brand new God.
Heal me, change me, make me brand new God.
Heal me, change me, make me brand new God.
Heal me, change me, make me brand new God.
Heal me, change me, make me brand new God.
Heal me, change me, make me brand new God.

Heal me, change me, make me brand new God.
Heal me, change me, make me brand new God.
Heal me, change me, make me brand new God.
Heal me, change me, make me brand new God.
Heal me, change me, make me brand new God.
Heal me, change me, make me brand new God.
Heal me, change me, make me brand new God.
Heal me, change me, make me brand new God.
Heal me, change me, make me brand new God.
Heal me, change me, make me brand new God.
Heal me, change me, make me brand new God.
Heal me, change me, make me brand new God.
Heal me, change me, make me brand new God.
Heal me, change me, make me brand new God.
Heal me, change me, make me brand new God.
Heal me, change me, make me brand new God.
Heal me, change me, make me brand new God.
Heal me, change me, make me brand new God.
Heal me, change me, make me brand new God.
Heal me, change me, make me brand new God.
Heal me, change me, make me brand new God.
Heal me, change me, make me brand new God.
Heal me, change me, make me brand new God.
Heal me, change me, make me brand new God.
Heal me, change me, make me brand new God.
Heal me, change me, make me brand new God.
Heal me, change me, make me brand new God.
Heal me, change me, make me brand new God.
Heal me, change me, make me brand new God.
Heal me, change me, make me brand new God.
Heal me, change me, make me brand new God.
Heal me, change me, make me brand new God.
Heal me, change me, make me brand new God.
Heal me, change me, make me brand new God.
Heal me, change me, make me brand new God.
Heal me, change me, make me brand new God.
Heal me, change me, make me brand new God.
Heal me, change me, make me brand new God.
Heal me, change me, make me brand new God.
Heal me, change me, make me brand new God.
Heal me, change me, make me brand new God.
Heal me, change me, make me brand new God.
Heal me, change me, make me brand new God.
Heal me, change me, make me brand new God.

Heal me
Heal me
Heal me
Heal me
Heal me
Heal me
Heal me
Heal me
Heal me
Heal me
Heal me,
Heal me,
Heal me,
Heal me,
Heal me,
Heal me,
Heal me,
Heal me,
Heal me,
Heal me,
Heal me,
Heal me,
Heal me,
Heal me,
Heal me,
Heal me,
Heal me,
Heal me,
Heal me,
Heal me,
Heal me,
Heal me,
Heal me,
Heal me,
Heal me,
Heal me,
Heal me,
Heal me,
Heal me,
Heal me,
Heal me,
Heal me,
Heal me,

Heal me, change me, make me brand new God.
Heal me, change me, make me brand new God.
Heal me, change me, make me brand new God.
Heal me, change me, make me brand new God.
Heal me, change me, make me brand new God.
Heal me, change me, make me brand new God.
Heal me, change me, make me brand new God.
Heal me, change me, make me brand new God.
Heal me, change me, make me brand new God.
Heal me, change me, make me brand new God.
Heal me, change me, make me brand new God.
Heal me, change me, make me brand new God.
Heal me, change me, make me brand new God.
Heal me, change me, make me brand new God.
Heal me, change me, make me brand new God.
Heal me, change me, make me brand new God.
Heal me, change me, make me brand new God.
Heal me, change me, make me brand new God.
Heal me, change me, make me brand new God.
Heal me, change me, make me brand new God.
Heal me, change me, make me brand new God.
Heal me, change me, make me brand new God.
Heal me, change me, make me brand new God.
Heal me, change me, make me brand new God.
Heal me, change me, make me brand new God.
Heal me, change me, make me brand new God.
Heal me, change me, make me brand new God.
Heal me, change me, make me brand new God.
Heal me, change me, make me brand new God.
Heal me, change me, make me brand new God.
Heal me, change me, make me brand new God.
Heal me, change me, make me brand new God.
Heal me, change me, make me brand new God.
Heal me, change me, make me brand new God.
Heal me, change me, make me brand new God.
Heal me, change me, make me brand new God.
Heal me, change me, make me brand new God.
Heal me, change me, make me brand new God.
Heal me, change me, make me brand new God.
Heal me, change me, make me brand new God.
Heal me, change me, make me brand new God.
Heal me, change me, make me brand new God.
Heal me, change me, make me brand new God.
Heal me, change me, make me brand new God.
Heal me, change me, make me brand new God.
Heal me, change me, make me brand new God.
Heal me, change me, make me brand new God.
Heal me, change me, make me brand new God.
Heal me, change me, make me brand new God.
Heal me, change me, make me brand new God.

Be Still

Be still child
Rest your weary bones
Be still child
The struggle's not all your own
Be still child
He's not ready to call you home

It's one of those nights
The kind that I ain't had in a while
It's been a struggle
But God always gave me reason to smile
Tonight God was slipping
Because the devil came through
Maybe it was test
A reminder
Child never let the devil shake you
Well I failed and I wailed
Praying the mental anguish would dissipate
It didn't
Every hour that passes equals another pill that I take
Benz 2 in counting
It's 2 in the morning
The rainy tears have finally stopped
Now it's just drizzling
Trem 6 in counting
I think I'm starting to feel the effects
My hands is getting shaky
My mind are slightly at rest

Sing myself to a chill place
A safe space
Be still my thoughts in this space
A blessed place

Be still child
You'll never be alone
Be still child
I'll be your refuge in this storm
Be still child
I'm not ready to call you home

It's one of those nights
The kind that I ain't had in a while
It's been a struggle
But God always gave me reason to smile
Tonight I must be tripping
Because an angel came through
This one had a message
Child be faithful in everything that you do
Difficult I know
Faith wears a little different on you
But wearing another's would be allowing your path
To become misconstrued
Don't be fooled
By all these wolves
Sheathed in sheep's wool
They'll whisper they mean you well
But have you playing the fool

When you find yourself in a strange place
Troubled space
Be still your thoughts in this space
A blessed place

Be still child
Rest your weary bones
Be still child
The struggle's not all your own
Be still child
He's not ready to call you home

Questions for Solomon

Many nights I sat here,
Lost and wondering.
Lord am I a burden?
Do you even want me?

Many nights I prayed,
Not knowing what would come.
Knowledge and understanding
What wise man ever truly won?

Solomon,
Did knowing so much
Cause you pain and drive you mad?
How does the wisest of men fall from grace?
How did you lose sight of God like that?

All these days in misery,
I kept one simple prayer.
Lord don't let me go.
I've lost my way again.

I know I asked for this,
And it's your will not mine.
But knowing so much more now,
Has my mind filled with strife.

Solomon,
Did you too need a distraction from your mind?
Is that how you came to have so many wives?
What shame(s) did you hide in the temples of false gods?
Was it worth it in the end? Was it everything you thought?

Healing

I've been working on healing
Every part of my soul
I asked God for direction
He said I had to let go

So I gathered all the pictures
Collected every memory
Tried to erase the parts I didn't like

I've been working on healing
Every part of my soul
I asked God for an answer
He kept saying let go

But I held on even tighter
Micro managed this and that
I hate feeling like I'm out of control

I've been working on healing
Every part of my soul
I asked God for forgiveness
He said He'd let it all go

I began to panic
Not fully understanding Him
Turns out it was me
Who could not forgive myself

I've been working on healing

Failing to See

You know those things you glimpse out the corner of your eye?
Maybe they're shadows, or orbs of light?
I see them all the time.
It's like they're spying on me.
I can feel them waiting on an answer I'm not sure I can give them.
Each time they start coming into focus
I drop what I'm doing and squeeze my eyes shut
So tight it hurts.
I pray and ask God to make them go away.
I shout at them to leave me alone.
I don't know what or who they are,
But I am terrified of what they could be.
A monster,
A demon,
A loved one,
An angel,
And angel trying to keep the demons at bay.
God I am so sorry...
I'm sorry
I keep failing to be brave enough.
I'm sorry
I give fear more attention then I give you sometimes.
I'm sorry
If I am missing something you are trying to show me.
I'm sorry
I am contradicting myself when I beg you to show me
that there is more than this
And then close my eyes when more appears.
God please don't give up on me.
Please hold my hand and walk by my side.
Give me the tools to fight the attacks on my mind.
Give me direction so that I may never be lost in fear again.
Forgive me for always asking so much of you,
I promise to do better.

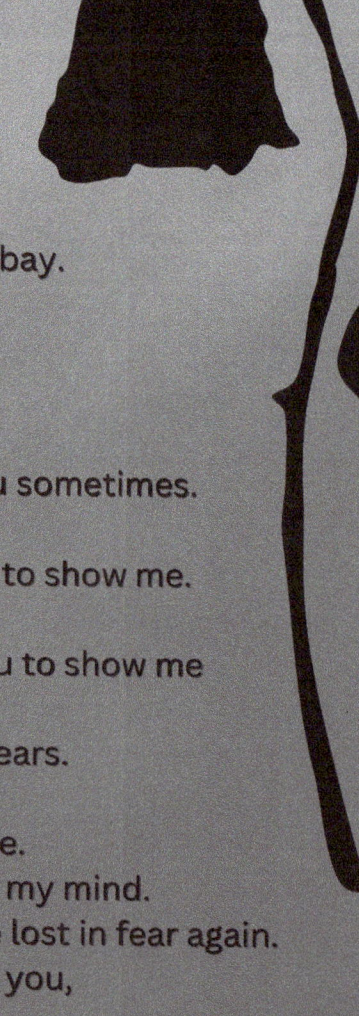

This Body of Mine

This body of mine
Has scars
Some are visible
Some are not
Some you can see up close and personal
Others you have to take a step back for

This body of mine
Holds pain
Like the moon holds water with a gravitational grip
Even when it's out of sight
I still feel tides of negative emotions
Rising to levels I can't stay afloat in
Waves crashing down and pulling me in all directions
Eroding my walls of sand that have kept my mind
Acceptably sunder

This body of mine
Heals slowly
The remnants of every struggle still on display
The chest tightens and breath shortens
The tongue numbs and throat swells
Any time Anxiety wins her ill timed attacks

This body of mine
Heals
Period
I need to remember that more often and be grateful
I need to pause when faced with new found pain
And remember that in time new wounds will heal
My body may hold pain like the memory of an Elephant
But a memory is not an open wound
And though it can scar
It can also fade

Mirror

Dear God,

When You created humans
We were beautifully and wonderfully made,
But I have yet to sense these things in myself
Or any proof of those remains.

It makes me wonder where am I?
If You are in everything then You are in me,
Therefore I should sense myself
In something other then me.

Or maybe I do,
I just don't like what I'm seeing.

Like in the algorithm of reality showing me everything I lack,
And the shrilling voice in my head telling me not to fight back.

Like in the greedy eyes of men as they prey on my flesh,
That tingle in my spine when we touch and say less.

Like in the taste of polluted air rolling in from the sea,
And the burn in my lungs when I'm struggling to breath.

Like in the pressures of mans religion crippling my bones,
And the grit in my teeth when they caution me "home."

God, when you gaze at Your reflection do YOU like what YOU see,
Or does the firmament of heaven distort the views we perceive.

Do You glare down at our flaws and think
Lord, where's the beauty and wonder?
Are You angry, are You sad,
How we've torn them asunder?

God, look into my eyes and do not hide your face.
For Yours is a wonder of beauty and grace.
A truth I pray I reflect one day...

Change my life for the better God.
Change my life for the better God.
Change my life for the better God.
Change my life for the better God.
Change my life for the better God.
Change my life for the better God.
Change my life for the better God.
Change my life for the better God.
Change my life for the better God.
Change my life for the better God.
Change my life for the better God.
Change my life for the better God.
Change my life for the better God.
Change my life for the better God.
Change my life for the better God.
Change my life for the better God.
Change my life for the better God.
Change my life for the better God.
Change my life for the better God.
Change my life for the better God.
Change my life for the better God.
Change my life for the better God.
Change my life for the better God.
Change my life for the better God.
Change my life for the better God.
Change my life for the better God.
Change my life for the better God.
Change my life for the better God.
Change my life for the better God.
Change my life for the better God.
Change my life for the better God.
Change my life for the better God.
Change my life for the better God.
Change my life for the better God.
Change my life for the better God.
Change my life for the better God.
Change my life for the better God.
Change my life for the better God.
Change my life for the better God.
Change my life for the better God.
Change my life for the better God.
Change my life for the better God.
Change my life for the better God.
Change my life for the better God.
Change my life for the better God.
Change my life for the better God.
Change my life for the better God.
Change my life for the better God.
Change my life for the better God.
Change my life for the better God.
Change my life for the better God.
Change my life for the better God.
Change my life for the better God.

Change my life for the better God.
Change my life for the better God.
Change my life for the better God.
Change my life for the better God.
Change my life for the better God.
Change my life for the better God.
Change my life for the better God.
Change my life for the better God.
Change my life for the better God.
Change my life for the better God.
Change my life for the better God.
Change my life for the better God.
Change my life for the better God.
Change my life for the better God.
Change my life for the better God.
Change my life for the better God.
Change my life for the better God.
Change my life for the better God.
Change my life for the better God.
Change my life for the better God.
Change my life for the better God.
Change my life for the better God.
Change my life for the better God.
Change my life for the better God.
Change my life for the better God.
Change my life for the better God.
Change my life for the better God.
Change my life for the better God.
Change my life for the better God.
Change my life for the better God.
Change my life for the better God.
Change my life for the better God.
Change my life for the better God.
Change my life for the better God.
Change my life for the better God.
Change my life for the better God.
Change my life for the better God.
Change my life for the better God.
Change my life for the better God.
Change my life for the better God.
Change my life for the better God.
Change my life for the better God.
Change my life for the better God.
Change my life for the better God.
Change my life for the better God.
Change my life for the better God.
Change my life for the better God.
Change my life for the better God.
Change my life for the better God.
Change my life for the better God.
Change my life for the better God.
Change my life for the better God.

Change my
Change my
Change my
Change my
Change my
Change my
Change my
Change my
Change my
Change my
Change my
Change my
Change my
Change my
Change my
Change my
Change my
Change my
Change my
Change my
Change my
Change my
Change my
Change my
Change my
Change my
Change my
Change my
Change my
Change my
Change my
Change my
Change my l
Change my l
Change my l
Change my l
Change my l
Change my l
Change my l
Change my l
Change my l
Change my l
Change my l
Change my l
Change my l
Change my l
Change my l
Change my li
Change my li
Change my li
Change my li
Change my li

tter God.
tter God.
tter God.
tter God.
tter God.
tter God.
tter God.
tter God.
tter God.
tter God.
tter God.
etter God.
etter God.
etter God.
etter God.
etter God.
etter God.
etter God.
etter God.
etter God.
etter God.
etter God.
etter God.
etter God.
etter God.
etter God.
etter God.
etter God.
etter God.
etter God.
etter God.
etter God.
etter God.
etter God.
etter God.
etter God.
etter God.
etter God.
etter God.
etter God.
etter God.
etter God.
etter God.
etter God.
etter God.
etter God.
etter God.
etter God.

Change my life for the better God.
Change my life for the better God.
Change my life for the better God.
Change my life for the better God.
Change my life for the better God.
Change my life for the better God.
Change my life for the better God.
Change my life for the better God.
Change my life for the better God.
Change my life for the better God.
Change my life for the better God.
Change my life for the better God.
Change my life for the better God.
Change my life for the better God.
Change my life for the better God.
Change my life for the better God.
Change my life for the better God.
Change my life for the better God.
Change my life for the better God.
Change my life for the better God.
Change my life for the better God.
Change my life for the better God.
Change my life for the better God.
Change my life for the better God.
Change my life for the better God.
Change my life for the better God.
Change my life for the better God.
Change my life for the better God.
Change my life for the better God.
Change my life for the better God.
Change my life for the better God.
Change my life for the better God.
Change my life for the better God.
Change my life for the better God.
Change my life for the better God.
Change my life for the better God.
Change my life for the better God.
Change my life for the better God.
Change my life for the better God.
Change my life for the better God.
Change my life for the better God.
Change my life for the better God.
Change my life for the better God.
Change my life for the better God.
Change my life for the better God.
Change my life for the better God.
Change my life for the better God.
Change my life for the better God.

Change my life for the better God.
Change my life for the better God.
Change my life for the better God.
Change my life for the better God.
Change my life for the better God.
Change my life for the better God.
Change my life for the better God.
Change my life for the better God.
Change my life for the better God.
Change my life for the better God.
Change my life for the better God.
Change my life for the better God.
Change my life for the better God.
Change my life for the better God.
Change my life for the better God.
Change my life for the better God.
Change my life for the better God.
Change my life for the better God.
Change my life for the better God.
Change my life for the better God.
Change my life for the better God.
Change my life for the better God.
Change my life for the better God.
Change my life for the better God.
Change my life for the better God.
Change my life for the better God.
Change my life for the better God.
Change my life for the better God.
Change my life for the better God.
Change my life for the better God.
Change my life for the better God.
Change my life for the better God.
Change my life for the better God.
Change my life for the better God.
Change my life for the better God.
Change my life for the better God.
Change my life for the better God.
Change my life for the better God.
Change my life for the better God.
Change my life for the better God.
Change my life for the better God.
Change my life for the better God.
Change my life for the better God.
Change my life for the better God.
Change my life for the better God.
Change my life for the better God.
Change my life for the better God.
Change my life for the better God.

Blue Dots

S	M	T	W	T	F	S
●	●	●	●	●	●	●
●	●	●	●	●	●	●
●	●	●	●	●	●	●
●	●	●	●	●	●	●
●	●	●	●	●	●	●
●	●	●	●	●	●	●

Fifty two blue dots on my calendar
Fifty two days of tears
Fifty two little reminders
Fifty two reasons I try not care

When I was 28 I was so convinced in my head that God was going to send me a husband and cure my lonely

When I was 28 I gave God every yes and followed my Lord wherever He lead me

When I was 28 I truly believed that if I asked God then I would receive
But 28 year old me was young and naïve

One hundred and thirteen blue dots on my calendar
One hundred and thirteen days of grief
One hundred and thirteen sour reminders
One hundred and thirteen days with no relief

I spent endless nights in my living room dancing the lonely and singing the blues

I grappled with the silence and coaxed the walls

I listened and waited for someone to respond

But nobody answered, not even God

One hundred and ninety eight blue dots on my calendar
One hundred and ninety eight days of tears
One hundred and ninety eight bitter reminders
One hundred and ninety eight days under a weight I couldn't bare

For weeks on end I spoke to no one and I disappeared in search of substance

The journey kept leading me back to my bed; the world was safer under the covers

I would close my eyes and fantasize about the perfect life under the sun

A life without pain or stress or strife and I was never alone

Two hundred and sixty two blue dots on my calendar
Two hundred and sixty two days of grief
Two hundred and sixty two heartbreaking reminders
Two hundred and sixty two days what I prayed for wasn't received

On my 29th birthday I felt so many emotions:
Anger, sadness, betrayal

I wept in bitterness then wept in joy because I was thankful
I made it this far

On my 29th birthday I made a decision
There will be no more blue dots on my calendar

So I swallowed my pain and buried it deep in the depths of my still aching heart

I'm So Blessed

I'm so blessed!
I have a roof over my head and my bills are paid.
I'm so blessed!
I have a car and it's paid off.
I'm so blessed!
I have a job with good benefits.
I'm so blessed!
I have friends and family that love me.

I'M SO BLESSED....I want to throw it all away out of frustration.

I'm so blessed but,
This roof over my head is part home, office, and isolation cell.
I'm so blessed but,
Paying off my car somehow didn't mean more room in the budget.
I'm so blessed but,
This so called great job works me to the point of mental breakage
and raises my blood pressure.
I'm so blessed but,
That same job has no steady schedule so I rarely get a life outside
of work to see friends and family or even go to church

But I'm so blessed!
I'm so BLESSED!
I'm SO blessed!

I'm SO tired.

Loving God

Loving God is harder than I thought it would be.

Because love is not the act of worshipping in church for approval
Or singing praise music louder than your sorrow

Loving God is harder than I thought it would it be

Because love is not the butterflies in your stomach
Or the person you ask to be your valentine

Loving God is harder than I thought it would be

Because I had heard love was patient, and love was kind
But there are times I am neither of those things

Loving God is harder than I thought it would be

Because loving is an action, a verb, a motion
And it's easy to be in love when the blessings are coming
But when they aren't?

Loving God is harder than I thought it would be

Because loving my God means loving His people
But I am not a people person
Lord make me a people person

Loving God is harder than I thought it would be

Because the people are lost in numerous ways
And so too am I
And I fear the Lord will say He never knew us
Because we could not find our way to meet one another

Bare with Me

Bare with me
I'm just thinking out loud
About...

All the little decision I made
And how my life turned out
How things could have been different
If I went right instead of left
And how it's stupid to reminisce on
Almost and could have been

I could drive myself crazy
With all the what ifs
If I had a dollar for all of them I'd be a
"What if" rich wench

Bare with me
I'm just thinking out loud
About...

How womens minds are like spaghetti
But I always preferred waffles
I like how the boys compartmentalize
Everything to the point it's unlawful

I wish I could put my emotions into little squares
So my anxiety was evenly dispersed and life
Would maybe feel a little less unfair

Cus I got
99 problems all left on read
I'll be sure to avoid messages before going to bed
The universe has no chill

Bare with me
I'm just thinking out loud
About...

Ten years in the future
Where and who I'll be
Did I settle for temporary comfort
Am I anything God said I would be

I'm second guessing my goals now
Over analyzing my why and the how

Like how did we get "here"

This is the question I'll ask my future children
Passing down the pressure of life's tragic illusion....

I need to stop thinking out loud

Healing is a Process

Healing is a process
Healing is a process
Healing is a process
Heal me God because I've been... tired

To the point I fear I may
Prematurely expire

I've only just begun to realize the magnitude
Of impact one event can have on life
I've been lying so well I believed I was fine
Not great or fantastic but I was doing alright
A few scars here and there but that all fades with time

Time heals all wounds
Let it heal you

I stopped taking care of myself
I stopped sleeping
I stopped asking people for help
I started retreating

I started eating myself to death
I started working my mind to ruins
I started thinking of myself as less
I stopped feeling human

Time heals all wounds
Let it heal you

Healing is a process
Healing is a process
Healing is a process
Heal me God because I've been... Trying?

Though somedays that's just doing the
Bare minimum of surviving

There is a shelf in my closet labeled skeletons
And lately it's begun to over flow

His, always finds a way to escape and fall down
Hitting the ground
Bones shattering all around

Making it harder to lie to myself... shit

I pick them up in haste
I slam them back into place
I hide Him far away in the darkest of space

But every time I try to heal or move forward
Never mind that it's either or
I am right back there with him

If cremation were an option
It would have been the only thing I
Willingly consented to
I would have burned away the mental images
The muscle memories too

There would be no bones to speak of
No bones in the graveyard
No bones to identify you...
No bones where it happened
You took my choice and my justice too...

Healing is a process
Healing is a process
Healing is a process
Heal me God because I've been... lonely

God I'm so lonely
I wish there were someone here
To come and hold me

But there isn't
Because I see red flags
Even when there are none
I push people away
Especially when I need them
Even more so when I want them

I can't be touched with out wanting
To crawl out of my own skin
I don't feel at home in my own skin

Because that night
Is an infinite loop in the back of my brain
Slowly, steadily, pushing me towards insane
So there's a constant stream of anger
Flowing through my veins

And I blame myself
When I should be blaming him
Then I start to hate myself more than I hate him
But that just makes the anger more potent
And causes me to spin

It's a vicious cycle
That always ends in tears
Which is why I've avoided this topic for past 5 years

But my will to move on
Is starting to outweigh all of my fears

Healing is a process
Healing is a process
Healing is a process
Heal me God because I don't...

Want to dwell in a
Perpetual state of fear
I am done cradling my grief
So my anger and sorrow
I'll leave them hear

And I will heal
Until every part of me
Knows peace

Lord make my heart brand new.
Lord make my heart brand new.
Lord make my heart brand new.
Lord make my heart brand new.
Lord make my heart brand new.
Lord make my heart brand new.
Lord make my heart brand new.
Lord make my heart brand new.
Lord make my heart brand new.
Lord make my heart brand new.
Lord make my heart brand new.
Lord make my heart brand new.
Lord make my heart brand new.
Lord make my heart brand new.
Lord make my heart brand new.
Lord make my heart brand new.
Lord make my heart brand new.
Lord make my heart brand new.
Lord make my heart brand new.
Lord make my heart brand new.
Lord make my heart brand new.
Lord make my heart brand new.
Lord make my heart brand new.
Lord make my heart brand new.
Lord make my heart brand new.
Lord make my heart brand new.
Lord make my heart brand new.
Lord make my heart brand new.
Lord make my heart brand new.
Lord make my heart brand new.
Lord make my heart brand new.
Lord make my heart brand new.
Lord make my heart brand new.
Lord make my heart brand new.
Lord make my heart brand new.
Lord make my heart brand new.
Lord make my heart brand new.
Lord make my heart brand new.
Lord make my heart brand new.
Lord make my heart brand new.
Lord make my heart brand new.
Lord make my heart brand new.
Lord make my heart brand new.
Lord make my heart brand new.
Lord make my heart brand new.
Lord make my heart brand new.
Lord make my heart brand new.
Lord make my heart brand new.
Lord make my heart brand new.
Lord make my heart brand new.
Lord make my heart brand new.
Lord make my heart brand new.
Lord make my heart brand new.
Lord make my heart brand new.

Lord make my heart brand new.
Lord make my heart brand new.
Lord make my heart brand new.
Lord make my heart brand new.
Lord make my heart brand new.
Lord make my heart brand new.
Lord make my heart brand new.
Lord make my heart brand new.
Lord make my heart brand new.
Lord make my heart brand new.
Lord make my heart brand new.
Lord make my heart brand new.
Lord make my heart brand new.
Lord make my heart brand new.
Lord make my heart brand new.
Lord make my heart brand new.
Lord make my heart brand new.
Lord make my heart brand new.
Lord make my heart brand new.
Lord make my heart brand new.
Lord make my heart brand new.
Lord make my heart brand new.
Lord make my heart brand new.
Lord make my heart brand new.
Lord make my heart brand new.
Lord make my heart brand new.
Lord make my heart brand new.
Lord make my heart brand new.
Lord make my heart brand new.
Lord make my heart brand new.
Lord make my heart brand new.
Lord make my heart brand new.
Lord make my heart brand new.
Lord make my heart brand new.
Lord make my heart brand new.
Lord make my heart brand new.
Lord make my heart brand new.
Lord make my heart brand new.
Lord make my heart brand new.
Lord make my heart brand new.
Lord make my heart brand new.
Lord make my heart brand new.
Lord make my heart brand new.
Lord make my heart brand new.
Lord make my heart brand new.
Lord make my heart brand new.
Lord make my heart brand new.
Lord make my heart brand new.
Lord make my heart brand new.
Lord make my heart brand new.
Lord make my heart brand new.
Lord make my heart brand new.
Lord make my heart brand new.
Lord make my heart brand new.

Lord make my hea
Lord make my hea
Lord make my hea
Lord make my hea
Lord make my hea
Lord make my hea
Lord make my hea
Lord make my hea
Lord make my hea
Lord make my hea
Lord make my hea
Lord make my hea
Lord make my hea
Lord make my hea
Lord make my hear
Lord make my hear
Lord make my hear
Lord make my hear
Lord make my hear
Lord make my hear
Lord make my hear
Lord make my hear
Lord make my hear
Lord make my hear
Lord make my hear
Lord make my hear
Lord make my hear
Lord make my hear
Lord make my hear
Lord make my hear
Lord make my hear
Lord make my hear
Lord make my hear
Lord make my hear
Lord make my hear
Lord make my hear
Lord make my hear
Lord make my hear
Lord make my hear
Lord make my hear
Lord make my hear
Lord make my hear
Lord make my hear
Lord make my hear
Lord make my hear
Lord make my hear
Lord make my hear
Lord make my hear
Lord make my hear
Lord make my hear
Lord make my hear
Lord make my hear
Lord make my hear
Lord make my hear

and new.	Lord make my heart brand new.	Lord make my heart brand new.
and new.	Lord make my heart brand new.	Lord make my heart brand new.
and new.	Lord make my heart brand new.	Lord make my heart brand new.
and new.	Lord make my heart brand new.	Lord make my heart brand new.
and new.	Lord make my heart brand new.	Lord make my heart brand new.
and new.	Lord make my heart brand new.	Lord make my heart brand new.
and new.	Lord make my heart brand new.	Lord make my heart brand new.
and new.	Lord make my heart brand new.	Lord make my heart brand new.
and new.	Lord make my heart brand new.	Lord make my heart brand new.
and new.	Lord make my heart brand new.	Lord make my heart brand new.
and new.	Lord make my heart brand new.	Lord make my heart brand new.
and new.	Lord make my heart brand new.	Lord make my heart brand new.
and new.	Lord make my heart brand new.	Lord make my heart brand new.
and new.	Lord make my heart brand new.	Lord make my heart brand new.
and new.	Lord make my heart brand new.	Lord make my heart brand new.
and new.	Lord make my heart brand new.	Lord make my heart brand new.
and new.	Lord make my heart brand new.	Lord make my heart brand new.
and new.	Lord make my heart brand new.	Lord make my heart brand new.
and new.	Lord make my heart brand new.	Lord make my heart brand new.
and new.	Lord make my heart brand new.	Lord make my heart brand new.
and new.	Lord make my heart brand new.	Lord make my heart brand new.
and new.	Lord make my heart brand new.	Lord make my heart brand new.
and new.	Lord make my heart brand new.	Lord make my heart brand new.
and new.	Lord make my heart brand new.	Lord make my heart brand new.
and new.	Lord make my heart brand new.	Lord make my heart brand new.
and new.	Lord make my heart brand new.	Lord make my heart brand new.
and new.	Lord make my heart brand new.	Lord make my heart brand new.
and new.	Lord make my heart brand new.	Lord make my heart brand new.
and new.	Lord make my heart brand new.	Lord make my heart brand new.
and new.	Lord make my heart brand new.	Lord make my heart brand new.
and new.	Lord make my heart brand new.	Lord make my heart brand new.
and new.	Lord make my heart brand new.	Lord make my heart brand new.
and new.	Lord make my heart brand new.	Lord make my heart brand new.
and new.	Lord make my heart brand new.	Lord make my heart brand new.
and new.	Lord make my heart brand new.	Lord make my heart brand new.
and new.	Lord make my heart brand new.	Lord make my heart brand new.
and new.	Lord make my heart brand new.	Lord make my heart brand new.
and new.	Lord make my heart brand new.	Lord make my heart brand new.
and new.	Lord make my heart brand new.	Lord make my heart brand new.
and new.	Lord make my heart brand new.	Lord make my heart brand new.
and new.	Lord make my heart brand new.	Lord make my heart brand new.
and new.	Lord make my heart brand new.	Lord make my heart brand new.
and new.	Lord make my heart brand new.	Lord make my heart brand new.
and new.	Lord make my heart brand new.	Lord make my heart brand new.
brand new.	Lord make my heart brand new.	Lord make my heart brand new.
brand new.	Lord make my heart brand new.	Lord make my heart brand new.
brand new.	Lord make my heart brand new.	Lord make my heart brand new.
brand new.	Lord make my heart brand new.	Lord make my heart brand new.
brand new.	Lord make my heart brand new.	Lord make my heart brand new.

A Letter from God

You say you dream of a future where your children do not have to walk on eggshells yet you do that with me...?

Why is that?
Are we not friends?
Am I not your Father?

Am I not the Great I Am who lovingly created you, sacrificed for you, provided for you?

You say my love is too tough, that you can not withstand it.
You move as though I have offended you, made things worse for you.

BUT I am a parent, so my love will be tough.

I am not a spirit bound by flesh so you can trust that my actions, my will, my love, will always be just.

You can not see what I see.
You can not comprehend what I know.

But know this... Daughter,
More is coming.

What I've shown you is coming.

You will wait,
You will learn patience.

What's for you will be.

Do not spend your nights crying and wondering...

Late Bloomer

I wonder if flowers ever get jealous of each other.

As the seasons change and each one begins to bloom,
there's always one bud that refuses to grow until all of the others
are swaying happily in the breeze.
I experience this and I think to myself, "Catch up little flower.
Grow faster...."

I talk to it and encourage its leaves to feed me information.
What do you need? Water, perhaps?
How can I help you? Are you getting enough sunlight?

Why are you so determined to stay closed off?

While the flower in wait may refuse to answer,
it is clear it is trying to blossom.
It may not happen for some time but its roots are strong.
Good things take time and if a flower can practice the art of
patience,
so too shall I.

Prayers & Answers

It bothers me
It bothers me
It bothers me

How everything I want is in reach
Yet it keeps missing me

Got on my knees and said my prayers
That's how this works right?

Then why is my blessing
Being felt everywhere
But in my life?

And it gets to me
It gets to me
It gets to me

That voice in my head
And it sings a song to me

"How bad do you want it?
Do you want this?
Do them dirty
F'em all
You's a bad ..."

NO

I tune it out
I tune it out
I tune it out

I filter and I concentrate
His words to mouth

I don't want to be that girl who
Trades her soul away

But I'm one crazy customer away
From a mental break

So I manifest
I manifest
I manifest

Wake up every day saying
I'll accomplish this

The millennial dream
To be my own boss
And to travel the world
Little to no cost

And then I pray
And I pray
And I pray again

I ask God to make it all
Make sense

And He reminds me
Of everything I've asked for

And now I'm overwhelmed
By everything I'm blessed with

But He warns me
"The struggle isnt over yet.
There's a lot to learn if you gon' be this type of blessed."

And so I meditate
I meditate
I meditate

Align my frequency
With everything that's meant for me

Because every generational curse
Will end here with me

From here forth only joy
Will touch my family tree

And see I get it
Ya I get it
Yes I get it now

When all is said and done
I shall wear a crown

Anointed in my
Blood, sweat and tears, this

Is the legacy I leave
To my future kids

Amen

The Yellow Dress

I had a vision I would one day wear a yellow dress

It wasn't the dress that was important
But rather what it would grow to represent

A homestead with a pond and family all around
A baby in my arms and children laughing
A joyful sound
A smile on my face and warmth in my heart
I felt it in my soul that this was Gods plan from the start

Year after year went by and I still had no yellow dress
I searched every site, brick and mortar but failed to find one
that fit

And when the blue dots came
Each one chipped at my faith
So I locked the vision in a memory box
Inside the furthest cell in my brain

Every so often I pull it out to reminisce
And now when I look at it, the eagerness has faded
There's no lingering bitterness
And I sense myself positively changing

I still want that yellow dress with colorful flowers
I still want a family, the warmth, and the joy
But there's no longer a time stamp, no pressure to find
That divine yellow dress meant for just the right time

Phases Continue

Right Now I'm in a reminisce
Then it starts to make me sad
But I'm in awe phase

An I'm not where I used to be
Thank God
But somedays I wish I was phase

Amazing how life goes
I can't help but shout and praise Him
I still have a ways to go
But my faith's no longer wavering

It's just

Phases

IKSYDK

I know something you don't know
Because God has placed it in my soul
What He tells me He may not tell you
Because we all got different jobs to do

I know something you don't know
Because God has placed it in my soul
Call me crazy call me out my mind
But that's what loving God looks like sometimes

5 x 55

Once I was daft and fragile
That ain't me no more
But when they look at me
I feel like all they see
Is a girl unhinged at her core

I am so annoyed
My mind's a web of confusion
Because I never knew what I could do
So I just kept on assuming

It's time to make some changes
Though they won't all approve
Trying to please everyone
Won't get things done
That's why I must push through

I'm a work in progress
And somedays I'll forget
How to ask for help
Or take care of myself
I'm human, I'll misstep

I am so frustrated
You won't see past my mistakes
If you could only see the queen that I will be
Then maybe you'd stop trying to mold me

It's time to make some changes
I didn't ask if you agreed
God said to do a thing
So that's what I'm doing
And I don't care what it cost me

Handed me fear and doubt
When I was younger that shaped me
But I'm a woman now and I will stand my ground
Go ahead, say that I'm crazy

It's time to make some changes
Approve or disagree
My God is on my side
So I will be alright
I'm just sad I can't take you all with me

5 x 55
Making sure my frequency and thoughts align
5 x 55
What's the prayer, now write it down, and visualize
5 x 55
Having faith that all my dreams will come to life
5 x 55
Daily affirmation that I'll be better then fine
5 x 55

Thank You In Advance

God,
I thank You for this amazing life You have blessed me with.

I asked for discipline and You gave me the will power and self control to be healthy in my body and mind and the obedience to listen when You speak.

I asked for knowledge
and You gave me the resources and skill sets I needed to grow in faith, spirituality, entrepreneurship, and leadership.

I asked for courage
and You gave me the strenth and bravery of a thousand men, ensuring no weapon formed against me will ever prosper.

I asked for wisdom
and You made me wise enough to lead and mentor a people into greatness so that generations after us will be prosperous long after we are gone.

God, I thank You.
God, I thank You.
God, I thank You.

In Jesus name,

AMEN!

Ecclesiastes 3:11

He Has Made All Things Beautiful In Its time.

Inlcuding You,
Wallflower.

Thank you God for this amazing life you have blessed me with.
Thank you God for this amazing life you have blessed me with.
Thank you God for this amazing life you have blessed me with.
Thank you God for this amazing life you have blessed me with.
Thank you God for this amazing life you have blessed me with.
Thank you God for this amazing life you have blessed me with.
Thank you God for this amazing life you have blessed me with.
Thank you God for this amazing life you have blessed me with.
Thank you God for this amazing life you have blessed me with.
Thank you God for this amazing life you have blessed me with.
Thank you God for this amazing life you have blessed me with.
Thank you God for this amazing life you have blessed me with.
Thank you God for this amazing life you have blessed me with.
Thank you God for this amazing life you have blessed me with.
Thank you God for this amazing life you have blessed me with.
Thank you God for this amazing life you have blessed me with.
Thank you God for this amazing life you have blessed me with.
Thank you God for this amazing life you have blessed me with.
Thank you God for this amazing life you have blessed me with.
Thank you God for this amazing life you have blessed me with.
Thank you God for this amazing life you have blessed me with.
Thank you God for this amazing life you have blessed me with.
Thank you God for this amazing life you have blessed me with.
Thank you God for this amazing life you have blessed me with.
Thank you God for this amazing life you have blessed me with.
Thank you God for this amazing life you have blessed me with.
Thank you God for this amazing life you have blessed me with.
Thank you God for this amazing life you have blessed me with.
Thank you God for this amazing life you have blessed me with.
Thank you God for this amazing life you have blessed me with.
Thank you God for this amazing life you have blessed me with.
Thank you God for this amazing life you have blessed me with.
Thank you God for this amazing life you have blessed me with.
Thank you God for this amazing life you have blessed me with.
Thank you God for this amazing life you have blessed me with.
Thank you God for this amazing life you have blessed me with.
Thank you God for this amazing life you have blessed me with.
Thank you God for this amazing life you have blessed me with.
Thank you God for this amazing life you have blessed me with.
Thank you God for this amazing life you have blessed me with.
Thank you God for this amazing life you have blessed me with.

Thank you God for this amazing life you have blessed me with.
Thank you God for this amazing life you have blessed me with.
Thank you God for this amazing life you have blessed me with.
Thank you God for this amazing life you have blessed me with.
Thank you God for this amazing life you have blessed me with.
Thank you God for this amazing life you have blessed me with.
Thank you God for this amazing life you have blessed me with.
Thank you God for this amazing life you have blessed me with.
Thank you God for this amazing life you have blessed me with.
Thank you God for this amazing life you have blessed me with.
Thank you God for this amazing life you have blessed me with.
Thank you God for this amazing life you have blessed me with.
Thank you God for this amazing life you have blessed me with.
Thank you God for this amazing life you have blessed me with.
Thank you God for this amazing life you have blessed me with.
Thank you God for this amazing life you have blessed me with.
Thank you God for this amazing life you have blessed me with.
Thank you God for this amazing life you have blessed me with.
Thank you God for this amazing life you have blessed me with.
Thank you God for this amazing life you have blessed me with.
Thank you God for this amazing life you have blessed me with.
Thank you God for this amazing life you have blessed me with.
Thank you God for this amazing life you have blessed me with.
Thank you God for this amazing life you have blessed me with.
Thank you God for this amazing life you have blessed me with.
Thank you God for this amazing life you have blessed me with.
Thank you God for this amazing life you have blessed me with.
Thank you God for this amazing life you have blessed me with.
Thank you God for this amazing life you have blessed me with.
Thank you God for this amazing life you have blessed me with.
Thank you God for this amazing life you have blessed me with.
Thank you God for this amazing life you have blessed me with.
Thank you God for this amazing life you have blessed me with.
Thank you God for this amazing life you have blessed me with.
Thank you God for this amazing life you have blessed me with.
Thank you God for this amazing life you have blessed me with.
Thank you God for this amazing life you have blessed me with.
Thank you God for this amazing life you have blessed me with.
Thank you God for this amazing life you have blessed me with.
Thank you God for this amazing life you have blessed me with.
Thank you God for this amazing life you have blessed me with.
Thank you God for this amazing life you have blessed me with.
Thank you God for this amazing life you have blessed me with.
Thank you God for this amazing life you have blessed me with.

Dear Wallflower

This is Your season to bloom.

To be as vibrant and as
fragrant As the peonies in
June.

To Kiss the sun and enjoy the
wind. Do not cling to the
question: If not now, when?

Dear Wallflower,

Always remember who you are.
Let all that is good in life Seep
deep into your roots and touch
your heart.

Because these are the perks of
being someone you love.
A fully bloomed flower no longer
a bud

These are the perks of growing
tall. With a stalk so strong

There's no need for a wall.

www.ingramcontent.com/pod-product-compliance
Lightning Source LLC
Chambersburg PA
CBHW041536120626

46551CB00019B/2721